HANDBOOK FOR STUDENT WRITING

Nell Ann Pickett
Ann Laster

Hinds Junior College

Canfield Press / San Francisco

A department of Harper and Row, Publishers

New York / Evanston / London

For our parents

Standard Book Number: 06–386801–6

Library of Congress Catalog Card Number: 78–172165

72 73 74 75   10 9 8 7 6 5 4 3 2 1

Preface

A *Handbook for Student Writing* is, as the title suggests, *for the student*. It was developed and written in an effort to provide a usable reference for the student writer. The material is presented simply and clearly with the emphasis on *what* to do rather than on what not to do. We have attempted to include those rules and procedures which student writers seem to ask about most often.

A comprehensive Glossary and Index make this handbook an easily used source for finding answers to questions that may arise during the writing process.

For their assistance in supplying specific information we are especially indebted to Mrs. Virginia Riggs and the staff of McLindon Library, Hinds Junior College; Ann Gallmeyer of the New Orleans Public Library; Barbara Carpenter of Tulane University; Lois Harris of Rebul Academy; and Retta Porter, Anne Hardy, Sandra Boyd, and Peggy Brent of Hinds Junior College. To Audrey Roth, Associate Professor of English, Miami-Dade Junior College, we are again grateful for her ever-objective, and ever-incisive, yet ever-patient, readings of the manuscript from its proposed to its final form.

N.A.P.
A.A.L.

Contents

HANDBOOK
FOR
STUDENT
WRITING

1
Approaches to Writing

All writing can generally be classified on the basis of its *purpose*, which may be to explain (Exposition), to narrate (Narration), to describe (Description), or to persuade (Argument).

Often, a single written piece utilizes more than one of these types at the same time. For example, narration may include description, explanation, and persuasion. The overall purpose of the writing may be to narrate an experience, but the writer, in accomplishing his purpose, may include the other types of writing.

This selection, from *Gift from the Sea* by Anne Morrow Lindbergh, illustrates the combination of the four types of writing.

"The Beach" from *Gift from the Sea**

The writer narrates her experiences as she vacations on the beach. She explains that the beach changes her apathy to a reawakened life. She describes, in paragraph 2, how the rhythms of the sea, the wind, the birds erase from her mind the cares of the world. In the last paragraph she tries to persuade herself (and the reader) that the sea rewards those who have patience and faith.

The beach is not the place to work; to read, write or think. I should have remembered that from other years. Too warm, too damp, too soft for any real mental discipline or sharp flights of spirit. One never learns. Hopefully, one carries down the faded straw bag, lumpy with books, clean paper, long overdue unanswered letters, fresh sharpened pencils, lists, and good intentions. The books remain unread, the pencils break their points, and the pads rest smooth and unblemished as the cloudless sky. No reading, no writing, no thoughts even—at least, not at first.

At first, the tired body takes over completely. As on shipboard, one descends into a deck chair apathy. One is forced against one's mind, against all tidy resolutions, back into the primeval rhythms of the seashore. Rollers on the beach, wind in the pines, the slow flapping of herons across sand dunes, drown out the hectic rhythms of city and suburb, time tables and schedules. One falls under their spell, relaxes, stretches out prone. One becomes, in fact, like the element on which one lies, flattened by the sea; bare, open, empty as the beach, erased by today's tides of all yesterday's scribblings.

And then, some morning in the second week, the mind wakes, comes to life again. Not in a city sense—no—but beach-wise. It begins to drift, to play, to turn over in gentle careless rolls like those lazy waves on the beach. One never knows what chance treasures these easy unconscious rollers may toss up, on the smooth white sand of the conscious mind; what perfectly rounded stone, what rare shell from the ocean floor. Perhaps a channelled whelk, a moon shell, or even an argonaut.

But it must not be sought for or—heaven forbid!—dug for. No, no dredging of the seabottom here. That would defeat one's purpose. The sea does not reward those who are too anxious, too greedy, or too impatient. To dig for treasures shows not only impatience and greed, but lack of faith. Patience, patience, patience, is what the sea teaches. Patience and faith. One should lie empty, open, choiceless as a beach—waiting for a gift from the sea.

EXPOSITION

Exposition intends to explain, that is, to make someone else know and understand as the writer does. It may give directions (to places, for recipes, for construction), express opinions and convictions, tell how something works or is organized (a machine, a city government, an industry), criticize, analyze, or interpret literary works and other art forms. Its evident purpose is to explain, inform, and instruct. Perhaps a better, more modern, word for it would be *explanation.*

Explanatory writing is used more often than any other form of writing. It is found in lectures, textbooks, newspapers, magazines, encyclopedias—all media whose primary purpose is to inform. The article, the essay, the letter, and the critique all use exposition.

Expository writing must be clear. If you wish to explain something, you must have a thorough knowledge of your subject; generally you should assume that the reader knows little of the subject you are explaining. Often, explanation includes specific examples and illustrations to help the reader understand the subject.

There are many possible methods for developing informative writing, and these will be discussed in great detail in Chapters 3 and 4. For now, some of the more common methods are:

> *Examples or illustration:* Explaining by giving specific instances to clarify general statements.
>
> *Definition:* Explaining by identifying the class an item belongs to and its distinguishing characteristics (that is, how it differs from other members of the same class). Extended definition may include description, examples, historical background or development, comparison and contrast, and analysis.
>
> *Comparison and contrast:* Explaining by showing similarities or differences between closely related items.
>
> *Cause and effect:* Explaining by analyzing the reasons for a given result.
>
> *Classification:* Explaining by recognizing similar characteristics among different items and sorting these items into related groups.

The following samples illustrate informative or explanatory

writing. First is a student theme "On Learning How to Cook," "A Burn: An Emergency" gives advice to the layman on how to treat burns, "Second Look" is a critical analysis of the movie *The Graduate*, and "Stanley Waldoff Plays a Memorable Recital" is a review of a piano concert.

Title states subject.

Paragraph 1 gives background information and introduces the main idea to be developed in the theme.

Paragraphs 2–14 use a detailed narrative account (includes specific examples) of a personal experience (a lengthy illustration) to explain how the writer learned to cook. Paragraphs 2–3 explain the writer's first mistakes at cooking the main courses for a meal.

On Learning How to Cook*

Let's say I was more or less forced into it when my mother went to the hospital for a major operation. Since Dad stays gone quite a bit on business trips, this left no one in the house except my sister and me to prepare meals. Having a fifteen-year-old sister seemed at the time like an advantage, for I felt cooking would be her department. Her first couple of meals were quite tasty. She called them "Sloppy Joes." By the third morning I asked myself how long a person could go on, just eating "Sloppy Joes." There seemed but one thing to do and that was to become chief cook in the Streetman household. Why couldn't I prepare the tasty meals my mother prepared? She never seemed to put out any effort.

I began to plan my first menu. I could picture a beautiful roast, baked potatoes, green beans, corn, and of course a salad. That sounded easy. I went to the freezer, selected a roast, picked my vegetables, and anticipated the superb meal. The roast was frozen awfully hard. Surely I needed a cookbook for a few answers.

According to the cookbook the meat should be thawed first. That would make dinner awfully late. Surely I could put it in a roaster and thaw and cook it at the same time. I placed it carefully in the roaster, looked at the buttons on the electric stove, and since I was in a hurry,

*Used by permission of Barbara Brooks Ingram.

Paragraph 4 shows a return of confidence as the writer follows cookbook instructions.

Paragraph 5 shows confidence wavering as she tries to select a potato recipe.

Paragraphs 6–7 explain that confidence as she prepares a salad.

pressed the button marked "High." Now for the vegetables. A pan for each. And again I pressed the "High" buttons. This all seemed relatively simple and I felt this would be a breeze. Since dinner was started, I opened the cookbook and searched for a special salad. I was deeply engrossed in the pictures of very complicated salads, when the most ghastly odor filled the room. I looked toward the stove and smoke billowed from a burned roast, burned corn, and burned beans.

Fortunately the roast was thick and the burned side could be trimmed off, but the corn and beans were a total loss. It was back to the freezer for other packages of corn and beans, and two more clean pans from the cabinet. I decided then to check the cookbook for instructions on how to prepare a roast, corn, and beans. According to the cookbook I was to brown both sides of the roast on a medium heat, cover and reduce to low. I was making progress!

I carefully followed the instructions for cooking the frozen corn and green beans. Since potatoes were on my menu, I decided to play it safe and do a little research in the cookbook before attempting to cook them. I had always taken potatoes for granted and had never given much thought to their preparation, so I was quite surprised when I found almost a whole chapter on recipes for cooking potatoes. There were recipes even mother had never prepared. I began slowly losing my confidence and decided for my first meal baked potatoes seemed the safest bet.

Everything seemed to be running smoothly so I decided to attempt a chef's salad. Who said cooking wasn't easy?

My confidence returned quickly. Anyone could chop up a head of lettuce. The tomatoes took a little more care. You sure couldn't grip them like a baseball. However, the onions were the crowning blow, when I found tears running down my cheeks. I would let Cheri and Dad select their favorite dressing. Since I had the salad under control, I decided to check on my roast and vegetables.

Paragraphs 8–9 show confidence wavering again as she checks the progress of the main course items and as she becomes aware of a sink of dirty dishes, pots, and pans.

Something was going wrong. The corn was done, the beans were almost ready, the potatoes in the oven were still hard as a rock, and the roast was still raw in the middle. I reached for the cookbook again and according to its chart, the roast would not be ready for another hour and a half, the potatoes should be ready in forty-five minutes and at the most, the beans could cook only ten more minutes. It made me wonder a bit how mother managed to have all of these things ready at the same time.

At the rate I was going we would have dinner at eight and I would have plenty of time to bake a cake. I looked at the sink and decided that some of the mess had to be cleaned up before I could start a new project. I was learning, too, that part of learning to cook involved quite a bit of scrubbing pots and pans.

Paragraph 10 reveals the writer's awareness of her inability as a cook as she selects a cake to bake for desert.

My selection of box cakes was limited and being an amateur cook, which I readily admitted by now, I decided a box cake was my safest bet. I followed the instructions carefully. I beat the batter exactly four minutes and it was sort of fun dripping it into the pan. Then came a whole new problem.

Paragraph 11 reveals new problems in the meal preparation.

I was baking potatoes at 375° and the instructions on the cake box called for 350°. It looked as though the cake was

Paragraphs 12–14 explain the results of the cooking experience.

going to have to wait until the potatoes were finished. The longer it sat, the less like cake batter it looked. With time on my hands once more, I thought ahead to breakfast. Bacon, eggs and toast would be a cinch after this.

After what seemed an eternity, the roast was done, or I should say overdone. It was falling apart. The corn had dried out, the beans didn't look much better, and the potatoes sounded as if they were encased in paper, but the cake was in the oven and would probably turn out fine. They always did for mother.

I quite proudly served Cheri and Dad a roast we couldn't slice, vegetables that looked old and shriveled, and terribly limp lettuce. In the middle of our meal the buzzer sounded on the oven and I dashed over to remove my cake.

Well, it didn't look like mother's. Hers always seemed to rise high in the pan. The cake was cooked but was just as shallow as when I put it in the oven. The directions said to run a knife around the edge of the pan and turn the cake out to cool before icing. It hit the cabinet with a thud and something told me this was not going to be the light, fluffy, moist cake they advertise on television. Dad and Cheri were most understanding and had to admit it was a change from "Sloppy Joes."

A Burn: An Emergency

A thermal burn (a direct heat burn from fire, contact with hot metal, or scalding) or an electrical burn (a burn from contact with electric current or by lightning) requires immediate treatment. Knowing what to do for a person receiving a burn may prevent the victim's suffering undue pain or even insure his survival.

For mild burns, burns producing reddening and blisters over a small area, apply cold compresses to the burned area. Mix a solution of two tablespoons of bicarbonate of soda to one quart of boiling water and allow to cool. Then, after soaking sterile gauze in the solution, place the gauze over the burn for twenty to thirty minutes. Dry the area carefully, and apply baby oil, petroleum jelly, or burn ointment; bandage firmly with a sterile compress covering the burned area.

For serious thermal or electrical burns, first, place the victim in a reclining position with his head lower than the rest of his body. Then, more than likely, you will need to treat the victim for possible shock. Keep him warm and quiet. Feed him a mixture of one pint of water, a half teaspoon of tablesalt, and a fourth teaspoon of bicarbonate of soda; continue to give him tea, coffee, or soft drinks. The important thing is to give him plenty of fluid to offset the loss of body fluids. If the victim experiences pain, give him two aspirin tablets with water containing a teaspoon of soda, or if it is available, give codein. As soon as possible remove the victim to a hospital.

For a severe burn, have the victim lie down. Attempt to cut away any clothing that remains around the burned area or areas. If the clothing sticks to the burn, do not remove it, for removal might cause internal bleeding, oozing, or shock. To protect the burned area, place additional layers of pads over the burn and bandage them firmly. Remember these "don'ts." Do *not* touch the burn with hands or clothing or absorbent cotton. Do not use an antiseptic or ointment. If possible, iron large handkerchiefs or pieces of sheet (or use the cleanest material available) and cover the burned area, holding the dressing firmly in place and bandaging to prevent external oozing and to support the weakened tissues. Then take time to send for a doctor or an ambulance. While waiting for the doctor or the ambulance, keep the patient warm. Offer him a solution of two tablespoons of soda to a quart of boiled water, a half glass at a time. If vomiting occurs, wait half an hour and offer the drink again. You can give aspirin or a sleeping tablet to relieve pain.

Second Look*

Paragraph 1 begins with a question to be answered according to the author's interpretation and analysis. Sentence 3 suggests that he will also compare the book and the film.

Doesn't the film split in half? This is the recurrent question in a number of letters about *The Graduate*—although almost all correspondents start by saying they enjoyed it! I have now seen it again

*Stanley Kauffmann, "Second Look," *The New Republic*, 1967.

and have read the novel by Charles Webb on which it is based, and some further comment seems in order.

I like what I liked in the film even more, but now, having read the original, I can see a paradox about its shortcomings. (Many of which were noted in my review.) Besides the fact that a great deal of Webb's good dialogue is used in the screenplay, the structure of the first two-thirds of his book—until Benjamin goes to Berkeley—is more or less the structure of the film. The longest scene in the picture —the one in which Benjamin tries to get his mistress to talk to him—is taken almost intact from the book. But Mike Nichols and his screenwriters rightly sensed that the last third of the book bogged down in a series of discussions that Webb's device for Benjamin's finding the place of Elaine's wedding was not only mechanical but visually sterile, and that in general this last third had to be both compressed and heightened. In reaction to the novel's weaknesses, they devised a conclusion that has weaknesses of its own. But there is a vast difference between weakness and compromise.

Benjamin does *not* change, in my view, from the hero of a serious comedy about a frustrated youth to the hero of a glossy romance; he changes *as Benjamin*. It is the difference between the women in his life that changes him. Being the person he is, he could not have been assured with Mrs. Robinson any more than he could have been ridiculous and uncommanding with Elaine. We can actually see the change happen—the scene with Elaine at the hamburger joint where he puts up the top of the car, closes the windows, and talks. *Talks*—for the first time in the film. Those

Paragraph 2 compares the structure of the book and the film. The reviewer's analysis reveals not only that the last third of the book is weak but also the devised film conclusion is weak.

Paragraph 3 analyzes the central character.

who insist that Mrs. Robinson's Benjamin should be the same as Elaine's Benjamin are denying the effect of love—particularly its effect on Benjamin, to whom it is not only joy but escape from the nullity of his affair and the impending nullity of himself.

There is even a cinematic hint early in the picture of the change that is to come. Our first glimpse of Mrs. Robinson's nudity is a reflection in the glass covering her daughter's portrait.

Paragraph 5 analyzes the story as it changes character emphasis and setting as they create problems in the screenplay.

In character and in moral focus the film does not split, but there is a fundamental weakness in the novel which the film tries, not quite successfully, to escape. The pivot of action shifts, after the story goes to Berkeley, from Benjamin to Elaine. From then on, he knows what he wants; it is she who has to work through an internal crisis. It was Nichols' job to dramatize this crisis without abandoning his protagonist, to show the girl adjusting to the shocking fact of Benjamin's affair with her mother, and to show it with, so to speak, only a series of visits by her to the picture. To make it worse, the environment—of the conventional campus romantic comedy—works against the seriousness of the material. The library, the quad, the college corridor have to be *overcome*, in a sense. Nichols never lets up his pressure on what he feels the film is about, but the obliqueness of the action and the associative drawbacks of the locale never quite cease to be difficulties. And, as I noted, the final chase—though well done—does get thin.

Paragraph 6 analyzes the film as a comedy and as a picture with depth.

But I think, with some viewers, Nichols also suffers from his virtues. He has played to his strength, which is comedy;

for, with all its touching moments and its essential seriousness, this is a very funny picture. A comedy about a young man and his father's partner's wife immediately seems adventurous; a comedy about a young man and a girl automatically gets shoved into a pigeonhole. This latter derogation seems to me unjust. We have only to remember (and to me it is unforgettable) that what is separating these young lovers is not a broken date or a trivial quarrel but a deep taboo in our society. For me, the end proof of the picture's genuine depth is the climax in the church, with Dustin Hoffman (even more moving the second time I saw him) screaming the girl's name from behind the glass wall. A light romance? That is a naked, last cry to the girl to free herself of the meaningless taboo, to join him in trying to find some possible new truth.

Paragraph 7 concludes with the reviewer's overall evaluation of The Graduate.

Yes, there are weaknesses. Yes, there are some really egregious gags. ("Are you looking for an affair?" the hotel clerk asks the confused Benjamin in the lobby.) But in the cinematic skill, in intent, in sheer connection with us, *The Graduate* is, if I may repeat it, a milestone in American film history.

Stanley Waldoff Plays a Memorable Recital*

Title and paragraph 1 state the reviewer's favorable reaction to the recital.

The only regrettable thing about the performance of Stanley Waldoff is that there were far too few people there to hear it. As for the ones who were there I am sure they will agree that it was a memorable recital.

*William Avera, [Jackson, Mississippi] *The Clarion-Ledger,* 17 April, 1971.

Paragraphs 2–3 identify the musical selections.

Although the recital was essentially one of nineteenth-century romantic music, it was well programed and served to point out the diversity of styles from the early to the late nineteenth century. The Schubert *G-Flat Impromptu Op. 90* and the Scriabin *Fourth Sonata* were the first two pieces and were, chronologically, the extremes of composers represented on the program. The remainder of the first half of the program was made up of two pieces from *Iberia, Book I* by Albeniz and the Mendelssohn-Liszt *Wedding March and Elfin Chorus.* After intermission Mr. Waldoff played the *B-Minor Sonata* of Chopin.

This was not a program of maudlin sentimentality but rather a program chosen by Mr. Waldoff from the age in which the piano and its literature reigned supreme in music and used by him as a vehicle for his remarkable pianistic and musical qualities.

Paragraphs 4–5 describe the pianist's performance.

The Schubert was played in a beautifully restrained singing style and the Scriabin was kaleidoscopic in coloring. The impressions of *Iberia* were subtly and evocatively wrought. Bravura playing was certainly one of the features of the nineteenth century and especially concerning the works of Liszt. Mr. Waldoff played the *Wedding March and Elfin Chorus* with all the verve, brilliance and audacity it deserved.

The Chopin *B-Minor Sonata,* like the rest of Mr. Waldoff's playing, was tightly knit, logical and clean piano playing. The third movement was especially remarkable for its beautiful voicing. For an encore Mr. Waldoff played the *F-Sharp Prelude* composed by his friend, Richard Cumming.

NARRATION

Narration tells a story or gives a series of related events. It may be a simple narrative, one in which events are set down in a natural time order (such as a biography, an incident, an anecdote, or an autobiography), or it may be as complex as a novel. Narration usually includes explanation to make the story or events understandable and description to provoke emotional or sensual response.

In narration the main emphasis is the action itself, the events taking place, the speech and actions of the characters. The order in which the material is presented is usually time, or chronological, order.

Perhaps, one day, you will write a short story, thus writing narration. Often, you will use narration as a way to support a central idea. That is, you will relate an experience as proof of a central idea. Such topics as my first day at college, finding a summer job, a visit to the mountains, catching the biggest fish in the pond, how I learned the value of money, and my favorite pastime offer opportunity for writing narration.

The following sample from *Newsweek* magazine uses a narrative approach.

Paragraph includes three events, arranged chronologically, with brief but specific facts about each.

Ten years ago last week, after a heavy snowfall had festooned Washington in white, *John Kennedy was inaugurated President.* The scene is graven into American political lore: an aging Robert Frost losing his place in the glare; a somber Dwight Eisenhower and his Cabinet muffled in great coats as the new Chief stood coatless to receive the oath, the word going forth that the torch had been passed to a new generation. *The "Kennedy years" had begun*—two years, ten months and two days during which the nation's and world's attention was fixed, as rarely before or since, upon a single family. *Then that other succession of images*, this time tinged with black: the muddled first bulletins from Dallas, a

riderless horse on Pennsylvania Avenue, a
flame flickering on an Arlington hillside.
Besides that flame and all the memories,
what else of the Kennedy years, at this
tenth anniversary of their beginning, endures?*

Here are two other samples using narration. The first is a narrative account of childhood experiences; the second is a narrative account of a student's experience with music.

Little Johnny Slept Here*

John pulled the car off the narrow country road in front of an
old deserted farmhouse. The cloud of dust that had been following us caught up and enveloped us. I grabbed the folded road map
and fanned myself in exasperation. The sun blazed down.

"Well," John said, "this is it. Let's go view the ruins."

"It's too hot. You go. I'll wait."

"Come on," he urged. "I'll show you where I used to hang my
sock for old Santa."

"Sail on!" I said impatiently. "Go ahead and get it over with."

John waded through the knee-high grass to the old house—
alone. While he was exploring his past, I sweltered and seethed in
the present.

We were on our way home from a month-long argument to California. This trip had been a sort of last-ditch attempt to save our
disintegrating marriage, with the unspoken understanding that if
harmony wasn't restored before we reached home, we'd go our
separate ways. We had not so much as touched each other, even
once, in the last three weeks, and we rode in the car like strangers
—he in his corner, I in mine.

John had set his goal in life and worked hard to reach it. When
his success was assured at last, I began to feel left out, neglected.
I thrive on affection and being needed. Without them I was
desolate.

"Come on in," he called from a broken window. "I just saw
Grandpa's ghost come down the stairs. No telling who you might
see here." He was trying to be gay. I pretended not to hear.

*From "The Kennedy Years: What Endures?" *Newsweek* (February 1,
1971). Copyright Newsweek, Inc., February, 1971.

*From "Little Johnny Slept Here" by Mrs. C. M. Williams, *Reader's Digest*
(February, 1971).

When John finally came back to the car, he was carrying a No Trespassing sign that had fallen over in the grass. "You're not going to take that thing home, I hope," I said. He didn't answer but took a pencil and printed on the sign. Then he went back, set it up in front of the old house—"LITTLE JOHNNY SLEPT HERE"—and again disappeared inside.

"Why?" I thought. "What's in there?" I was broiling in the car. I got out and made my way through the tall, dusty grass.

When I entered the house, John was just standing there, amid dust and cobwebs and bits of broken plaster fallen from the ceiling. This was the parlor that was also a bedroom when company came, he said. A bed had stood in the corner, with a headboard as high as his grandfather. The pillows always stood up, and were covered by square pillow shams with peacocks in bright-colored cross-stitch.

We went to the kitchen. He showed me where the old cookstove used to stand, and the woodbox that he'd filled for Grandma so many times. And the kitchen table. "It was covered with oilcloth," he said, "oilcloth with pansies on it. The prettiest pansies I ever saw."

Upstairs, we entered a big, forlorn-looking room with one tall window. "I used to lie on the bed here and imagine that window reached right up into the sky."

"I understand now why you wanted to come back here," I said. "It was home to you, wasn't it?"

"No. Not home. Just a here-today-gone-tomorrow sort of place. I was too much for the old folks. I'd be here a few weeks, then an aunt or uncle would take me over for a while. Wherever I happened to be, my suitcase was always under the bed, waiting to go when they tired of me. I probably was a nuisance.

"One time I was visiting my cousins. There was a row of clothes hooks on the wall, just our height. Each one had a name under it, and no one dared to use another's hook. Gee, I thought, if only I had a hook all my own like my cousins had! I finally found one and asked Aunt Millie, 'Could I please put my name under the empty one?' 'Oh, you won't need it,' she told me. 'You won't even be here next week.' I ran out on the porch and howled and howled until she made me stop it.

"Another time, my cousin Curt hurt himself. Aunt Millie gathered him up in her lap to bandage his toe, and held him for a while to stop his crying. I remember standing by the door watching; it seemed to me the most wonderful thing in the world to have a mother hold you close while she bandaged your toe, and say, 'Never mind. Everything's going to be all right.'

"I guess that's what I've really wanted, all my life. Someone to hold me when I was hurt or lonely; a place to live that was *my* home, this week and next week and always; and my own hook to hang my coat on."

John sat on the dusty windowsill and pulled me down beside him. He was almost casual as he related his story, but the vivid picture that came through tore at my emotions and wrenched me out of the cocoon of self-pity I had been weaving around myself. I was watching a lonely, motherless six-year-old, in this very room, a long time ago. Suddenly that boy was very dear to me.

I could hear the winter winds rattling the windows of the old farmhouse, and, peering out through the frosted panes, just as he had then, I could see the moon. It gave the lonely little fellow the only comforting light in the dark, shivery room and seemed his only friend.

This evening Grandpa had said to Aunt Alice, "We'll bring the boy over in the morning. He's big enough to fetch in the wood for you. I'll come for that calf next week."

So he'd been traded off, he assumed, for a calf. He'd never again get to sit for hours in Grandpa's beautiful black buggy, and pretend he was driving a team of prancing black horses. The buggy would still have its own special place, there between the corn bin and the horse stall. *It* had a home. Only little boys were traded like calves.

Almost lost in his grown uncle's nightshirt, the boy crawled out of bed and tiptoed over the cold floor to the window. He stuck his forefinger in his mouth to make it warm and wet, then rubbed it against the frosted pane to clear a spot through which to see. He looked up at the moon and his small body shivered. "Please, Mr. Man-in-the-Moon," he pleaded, "don't let Grandpa trade me off. *Please* let me stay."

"I bawled myself to sleep that night," the man beside me said, and chuckled as if it were funny.

When he finally stopped talking, I found that my hand had somehow stolen into his, and I was grasping it tightly. But it was not just the hand of my husband I was holding so protectively; it was also the hand of a very small, very frightened, heart-broken little boy.

Never again was I able to look at John without seeing, too, a reflection of the little fellow who wanted only a hook to hang his coat on, a place to call home—and someone to reassure him when he stubbed his toe. Now, I realized that I had no monopoly on the need for affection and reassurance. And, with a new serenity, I could understand his *intention*, and that this was what really counted.

Now when he said, "Get your war paint on. Let's go for a ride," I knew it was his way of saying, "I love you. Come share the big outdoors with me." Or when we'd planned to visit friends for the evening, and he suddenly said, "Let's just sit here on the porch instead, and listen to the rain on the roof," I knew he meant, "I'd rather be at home alone with you than anyplace else in the world."

As John and I rode down that dusty country road away from the old house, we turned a corner into a different life. In the years that followed, there grew a nearness and dearness between us. When irritation tempted me to be impatient, or when I knew things were going wrong for him, I'd quietly slip my hand in his. "Never mind. Everything will be all right." No matter how tense the situation, his response was always the same—a tightening of his hand on mine.

And then one day, John suffered a severe cerebral thrombosis, after which he did not move again, and seemed to be in a coma. As I rode beside him in the ambulance on the way to the hospital, I clasped his hand firmly in mine, and spoke clearly, "Never mind, dear. Everything will be all right."

His staring eyes focused on my face for one brief instant, and I felt a perceptible tightening of his hand.

Was it a split second of awareness, or just a reflex response? I do not know. But I like to believe that in that moment, he knew, if ever so briefly, fulfillment of his lifetime need of love and re-assurance.

My Musical Ability*

Paragraph 1 introduces main idea.

While his buddies were in Korea for the war, my father was a civilian touring the night clubs and bars that circled the Mediterranean Sea. But instead of merely having a good time, my father was entertaining the guests by playing the drums. Ever since I can remember, I have known that my father was a drummer, and so I

*Used by permission of Rob Hamilton.

Paragraphs 2–6 give specific examples (personal experiences arranged chronologically) to prove "became obsessed with being a musician."

became obsessed with being a musician.

My first passion was the ukulele. For years I begged for a ukulele. I finally got one, then immediately broke it and forgot about it.

Next was a guitar. When I bought one, I proudly took it home to show my parents, then set it in my room as a decoration for three years. Eventually I learned to play the guitar, and then my parents started casting evil looks my way and muttering something about "damn hippies." I couldn't understand it.

About this time I entered junior high school and joined the band. I took a few lessons on the alto clarinet, mainly because no one else would, and learned how to play and read music. From here it was simple to switch to the bass clarinet.

The summer before I entered high school, the band director handed me a bassoon and said, "Learn." So I took the bassoon and a fingering chart home and taught myself the bassoon and the bass clef. There is a certain status in being able to play the bassoon because few people know what it is.

Once I saw that I could conquer the bassoon on my own, I became power-mad. I wanted to play everything. Pretty soon I had mastered the drums, both the acoustic and the electric bass, the saxophone, and the piano. Smugly, I sat on my rear to await the recording companies.

Paragraphs 7–9 conclude that "obsession" isn't enough motivation for becoming a skilled musician.

But they didn't come.

While I was wondering why, I noticed that every other musician I knew was working on his same old instrument. Then I noticed that they were *good*, really good! And I wasn't particularly good on anything. . . .

Now I've realized that I should go back and relearn every instrument so that I will have some measure of skill. Right now I couldn't earn a glass of water in one of those Mediterranean bars.

Moral: You can own a mountain of gold, but if you only sit on it, the housewife's cabbage patch is more valuable.

DESCRIPTION

Description appeals to the senses: seeing, hearing, tasting, smelling, and feeling. Most often it appeals to seeing and hearing. Descriptive writing is an attempt to put into words sense impressions, a mood, or an atmosphere. It deals with hardness or softness, heat or cold, odors, colors, sights, shapes, noises, dimensions, roughness or smoothness, cowardice or bravery—any experience that involves response through the senses. It can describe an object, a person, a place, an incident, or a feeling (such as anticipation, fear, happiness).

Writing description is a highly selective process. It requires a careful selection of details that call up vivid, clear-cut images and striking impressions. The order in which descriptive material is presented is generally space order; it may also be arranged in the order of climax, of dominant feature, or degree of appeal to the writer.

Following is a selection from Theodore Dreiser's *Sister Carrie;** notice the descriptive details (italicized).

Here was a type of the travelling canvasser for a manufacturing house—a class which at that time was first being dubbed by the slang of the day "drummers." He came within the meaning of a still newer term, which had sprung into general use among Americans in 1880, and which concisely expressed the thought of one whose dress or manners are calculated to elicit the admiration of susceptible young women—a "masher." *His suit was of a striped and crossed pattern of brown wool,* new at that time, but since become familiar as a business suit. *The low crotch of the vest revealed a stiff shirt bosom of white and pink stripes. From his coat sleeves protruded a pair of linen cuffs of the same pattern, fas-*

*Theodore Dreiser, *Sister Carrie.*

tened with large, gold plate buttons, set with the common yellow agates known as "cat's eyes." His fingers bore several rings—one, the ever-enduring heavy seal—and from his vest dangled a neat gold watch chain, from which was suspended the secret insignia of the Order of the Elks. The whole suit was rather tight-fitting, and was finished off with heavy-soled tan shoes, highly polished, and the grey fedora hat. He was, for the order of intellect represented, *attractive*, and whatever he had to recommend him, you may be sure was not lost upon Carrie, in this, her first glance.*

Below are two student themes. The first describes impressions of the countryside in parts of California; the second uses descriptive details to show how smells recall memories.

From Merced to Yosemite*

Paragraph 1 introduces central idea.

An event that stands out in my mind is a trip I took along with some of my relatives through part of the state of California. Our destination on this journey was magnificent Yosemite National Park.

Paragraphs 2–6 are a narrative account of the trip with major emphasis on description of the countryside.

We began our trip toward Yosemite from a little town in northern California called Merced. Just outside Merced the land was very flat and very dry. Tall, shaggy, dusty, yellow weeds grew all along the highway and covered most all the open land I could see. I saw old, worn-out pieces of farm machinery here and there that had probably been used to convert patches of farmland. I found the area outside of Merced very depressing and lonely.

Gradually, these weed-covered patches began giving way to gently sloping foothills covered with short, golden, silky prairie grass. Looking out from the car as we drove along, I could see the wind making V-shaped patterns through the top of the grass like a little fish swimming swiftly just below the surface of a still

*Used by permission of Martin Davis.

mountain lake. As I admired these golden foothills stretching as far as the eye could see, I wished I was travelling through by horseback rather than in a "horseless carriage."

Eventually we emerged from these foothills into an area covered by low-lying, rocky, dusty mountains. As I looked at these mountains, I thought how easy it would be to just walk right up to the top of any one of them. But as I compared the size of a giant cactus that had just hurried past my window with the seemingly small size of one of the same kind near the top of one of those mountains, I realized it would be quite a task to just walk right up there..

Suddenly, my eyes were taken off this lonely cactus on the mount and were focused on a sparkling mountain stream that had just appeared along the highway very near the car. I was told that we were nearing Yosemite. As I heard this, I noticed the mountains had moved up closer to the highway. And surprisingly enough, their looks had changed. No longer were there dusty-brown, rounded mountains loafing along the highway; these had been replaced by high walls of rock standly proudly just across the stream and announcing that their magnificent brothers were just ahead, guarding beautiful and quiet Yosemite Valley.

Then, almost instantly, we were at the entrance to Yosemite National Park. This entrance was not a man-made passageway but a grand doorway to unwordly beauty created by Mother Nature herself. We passed between two steep cliffs. As I looked in awe at the sight now before me, I saw gigantic mountains towering straight up like icebergs in the North Sea.

As far as I could see all around me, Nature's majestic guardians stared down upon me. The valley floor about me was covered with friendly trees which seemed to welcome me with cool, swaying arms. And still, above and through the tree-tops, I could see the guardians; magnificent, bold, unyielding for centuries; looking, staring out across years of proud eternity; challenging me to name another thing in creation so beautiful. Soft, velvet waterfalls waved to me as they cleansed the faces of the mountains from which they came. On top of the mountains about me, I could see an occasional oak tree which had grown straight up half-way and then had bent back down to receive her oxygen because there was none where her lofty head should have been. I felt sorry for her and her lonely distant comrades.

As I think about all this grandeur, all this magnificence, God's very work of creation unspoiled since the beginning of time, I have a great desire to travel that road from Merced to that heaven on earth once again. From Merced to Yosemite—that is an experience I will never forget.

Paragraph 7 is personal comment on the effect of the trip.

Smells*

Paragraph 1 introduces central idea.

Certain smells have a way of passing through my nose and embedding themselves in my memory. Different experiences that are long forgotten can suddenly come back when an odor is present.

Paragraph 2 identifies specific smells and the experiences each recalls.

My first grade teacher, for example, wore a kind of perfume that always reminded me of dishwater. Now, whenever I smell dishwater, I think of my

*Used by permission of Richard Lowery.

first grade teacher. My first grade classroom usually smelled like crayons and Play-doh. Nowadays, when I smell crayons and Play-doh, an image of my first grade classroom comes to my mind. A wonderful combination of fragrances is that of Play-doh, crayons, and dishwater: the moment I realize that I am smelling these three smells together, I become crazy and forget how to multiply and divide.

Sentence 1 restricts topic to smells that signal events about to happen. Sentences 2–3 identify a specific smell and the experience it recalls,

Some smells can call back other kinds of memories and signal events about to happen. A perfect example of a smell that signaled an event was the clean, military smell of my father's seabag and jungle gear. Every time I smelled seabags and jungle gear, my father would go overseas or the whole family would move together.

Sentences 1–2 restrict topic to smells, usually of natural things, that recall certain times. Sentences 3–4 identify specific smells and the times they recall.

There are smells that remind me of certain periods of my life. Usually, these are the smells of natural things. The smell of cow dung always reminds me of March and April in Hawaii, when prevailing winds blow from the ranches around Haleakala crater. The odor of any natural thing, such as a flower, brings to mind early spring in the Wasatch Mountains.

Sentences 1–2 restrict topic to a smell that recalls a "bad memory." Sentence 3 identifies the smell and the experience it recalls.

Most smells remind me of pleasant experiences in different places. There is only one smell that can recall any sort of bad memory—the smell of the military. I always noticed that Marine Corps headquarters smelled the same: seabags, jungle gear, and stale coffee. For some reason, this smell always frightened me.

Paragraph 10 is personal comment on the importance of smells.

Smells always seem to stay in my mind long after people and places disappear. One day, no doubt, I'll start remembering people by their smell only, without ever trying to learn a name.

This excerpt from Poe's "Fall of the House of Usher" illustrates description of a mood and an atmosphere. The narrator, in the beginning paragraph, reveals apprehension; by the end of paragraph 4 this apprehension has grown into sheer terror. Poe creates this changing mood or atmosphere through the use of vividly descriptive words, strong punctuation (dashes and exclamation points), contrast of long and short sentence lengths which helps to heighten the uncertain feeling of the narrator, and inverted sentence patterns. The combination of these techniques points up the narrator's and Usher's near hysterical state.

From Poe's "Fall of the House of Usher"*

It was, especially, upon retiring to bed late in the night of the seventh or eighth day after the placing of the lady Madeline within the donjon, that I experienced the full power of such feelings. Sleep came not near my couch—while the hours waned and waned away. I struggled to reason off the nervousness which had dominion over me. I endeavored to believe that much, if not all of what I felt, was due to the bewildering influence of the gloomy furniture of the room—of the dark and tattered draperies, which, tortured into motion by the breath of a rising tempest, swayed fitfully to and fro upon the walls, and rustled uneasily about the decorations of the bed. But my efforts were fruitless. An irrepressible tremor gradually pervaded my frame; and, at length, there sat upon my very heart an incubus of utterly causeless alarm. Shaking this off with a gasp and a struggle, I uplifted myself upon the pillows and, peering earnestly within the intense darkness of the chamber, hearkened—I know not why, except that an instinctive spirit prompted me—to certain low and indefinite sounds which came, through the pauses of the storm, at long intervals, I knew not whence. Overpowered by an intense sentiment of horror, unaccountable yet unendurable, I threw on my clothes with haste (for I felt that I should sleep no more during the night) and endeavored to arouse myself from the pitiable condition into which I had fallen, by pacing rapidly to and fro through the apartment.

I had taken but few turns in this manner, when a light step on an adjoining staircase arrested my attention. I presently recognized it as that of Usher. In an instant afterward he rapped, with a gentle touch, at my door, and entered, bearing a lamp. His countenance

*Edgar Allan Poe, *"Fall of the House of Usher."*

was, as usual, cadaverously wan—but moreover, there was a species of mad hilarity in his eyes—an evidently restrained *hysteria* in his whole demeanor. His air appalled me—but anything was preferable to the solitude which I had so long endured, and I even welcomed his presence as a relief. . . .

No sooner had these syllables passed my lips, than—as if a shield of brass had indeed, at the moment, fallen heavily upon a floor of silver—I became aware of a distinct, hollow, metallic, and clangorous, yet apparently muffled, reverberation. Completely unnerved, I leaped to my feet; but the measured rocking movement of Usher was undisturbed. I rushed to the chair in which he sat. His eyes were bent fixedly before him, and throughout his whole countenance there reigned a stony rigidity. But, as I placed my hand upon his shoulder, there came a strong shudder over his whole person; a sickly smile quivered about his lips; and I saw that he spoke in a low, hurried, and gibbering murmur, as if unconscious of my presence. Bending closely over him, I at length drank in the hideous import of his words.

"Now hear it?—yes, I hear it, and *have* heard it. Long—long—long—many minutes, many hours, many days, I have heard it—yet I dared not—oh, pity me, miserable wretch that I am!—I dared not —I *dared* not speak! *We have put her living in the tomb!* Said I not that my senses were acute? I *now* tell you that I heard her feeble first movements in the hollow coffin. I heard them—many, many days ago—yet I dared not—*I dared not speak!* And now—tonight—Ethelred—ha! ha!—the breaking of the hermit's door, and the death-cry of the dragon, and the clangor of the shield!—say, rather, the rending of her coffin, and the grating of the iron hinges of her prison, and her struggles within the coppered archway of the vault! Oh, whither shall I fly? Will she not be here anon? Is she not hurrying to upbraid me for my haste? Have I not heard her footstep on the stair? Do I not distinguish that heavy and horrible beating of her heart? Madman!" Here he sprang furiously to his feet, and shrieked out his syllables, as if in the effort he were giving up his soul—*"MADMAN! I TELL YOU THAT SHE NOW STANDS WITHOUT THE DOOR!"*

ARGUMENT

The purpose of argument is to persuade, to convince the reader to accept a stated proposition by presenting a writer's substantiated opinion on a question. It intends to form or to change beliefs, theories, or policies and to influence the reader to act accordingly. Argument usually includes support from one of the other forms of writing.

To write a persuasive paper, you must first identify the central idea or proposition the paper will develop. Then select specific materials to support your argument and arrange these in an order that best presents the argument. These materials should include both logical and emotional appeal.

The two methods of logical reasoning are inductive and deductive. Inductive reasoning is known as the scientific method. It proceeds from a set of observed facts to a general conclusion (particular to general). For example: Everytime I walk through a certain woods area, I break out with poison ivy (observed fact). There must be poison ivy in that area (conclusion). Deductive reasoning proceeds from a generalization to the particular. It involves three steps: a statement assumed to be true presents a general classification, a particular fact is presented as a part of the general classification, a conclusion is reached on the basis of the preceding. For example: All persons entering college must have taken the ACT test (general truth). Joe is entering college (particular). Joe has taken the ACT test (conclusion).

The following samples illustrate persuasion as an approach to writing.

New Cities*

Sentence 1 states the central idea or proposition. Sentences 2–3 expand the proposition.

America cannot afford over the next few decades to concentrate another 50 million or more people in very large metropolitan centers. Already too many Americans feel themselves imprisoned by the city.

So we must plan now for an America that offers a free choice of a good life everywhere—in the inner city, in the suburbs, in new rural towns, in small rural communities, and on the farm.

*Orville L. Freeman, Former U.S. Secretary of Agriculture. Reprinted from *The Progressive Farmer*, copyrighted March 1971.

Paragraphs 3–4 offer suggestions for changing the condition stated in the proposition.

We need a national policy for the development of new cities in the countryside—new cities that offer their own sources of employment, esthetic satisfaction, and ample cultural, social, and recreation facilities.

I can't tell you how many new cities should be built. We must develop a total national plan to do that. But I will predict that such a plan will call for eight to a dozen new centers of 100,000 to 250,000 population each, placed strategically along the length of Appalachia. They will be tied to the metropolitan areas of the eastern quarter of the nation by new, comfortable, fast trains. Thus, people will be able to enjoy the best of both worlds living close to the country and still having access to opportunities that only a metropolis can provide.

Fluoridation: Still an Urgent Need*

Paragraph 1 identifies speaker and states his proposition that fluoridation is a basic public health need.

When I was Surgeon General of the U.S. Public Health Service, I spoke often of fluoridation as a basic public health need. I felt then, and do now, that all our children should have as their birthright the full benefit of this health measure.

Paragraph 2 explains the reason for his concern.

Yet still today, millions of American children suffer from tooth decay; dentists still fill and replace teeth that could have been saved by fluoridation. In too many areas of the country, an entire generation has grown up with an accumulation of dental ills that could have been prevented. I find these facts very disturbing —and so should every American parent.

*Luther Terry, M.D., "Fluoridation: Still an Urgent Need," guest editorial in *Parents' Magazine*, November 1970, © 1970 Parents' Magazine Enterprises, Inc.

Paragraphs 3–6 give specific facts to support the proposition.

Twenty-five years have passed since the fluoridation of public water supplies began in this country. Experience over that quarter century reveals that fluoridated water prevents up to two-thirds of the tooth decay that children would ordinarily suffer. Furthermore, it is medically safe for people of all ages—and its benefits last for a lifetime.

Fluoridation has paid off dramatically in dental bill savings. A new study in Newburgh, New York, a city fluoridated since 1945, disclosed that five- and six-year-old children from low-income families had only half the dental defects of their counterparts in the fluoride-deficient neighboring city of Kingston. Newburgh youngsters required half the dentists' time and less than half the money to treat. (This same study underlines the special importance of fluoridation to disadvantaged children, who often lack the other elements of good dental health—adequate diet, good home care, and regular dental checkups.)

Fluoridation is now standard water-treatment practice in 7500 communities in the United States. New York City, Chicago, Detroit, Washington, D.C., Miami, San Francisco, Philadelphia, Pittsburgh, Cleveland, Dallas, Atlanta, Denver, and St. Louis are all fluoridated cities. And state laws now make it required in Connecticut, Illinois, Minnesota, Delaware, Michigan, Ohio ,and South Dakota.

In this ecology-conscious age, it's interesting to note that fluoridated water is a natural component of the environment in many parts of our country. Generations of our forefathers used naturally fluoridated water before the fluoride itself was discovered to be the reason for their good teeth. In research on the people living in these naturally fluoridated communities, both the effectiveness and the safety of fluoridation were proved. And so, even before fluorides were first added to water systems 25 years ago, we were confident of the results. It seems ironic, then, that at a time of high public interest in the environment, many communities are passing up a perfectly natural health measure.

Paragraphs 7–8 give reasons why others have not supported the proposition.

And why, if fluoridation is so effective, is it still lacking in half the public water supplies in this country? The reason is simple: fluoridation depends upon political action for its beginning in a community. The political action may be a decision of the mayor or city council, a referendum, or a vote of the state legislature. The progress of no other public health measure—immunization against disease, pasteurization of milk, and so on—has had to depend upon the vote of citizens.

Public opinion polls show that most people favor fluoridation, but a number are uncertain of what it means, and too many others are apathetic about voting on a dental health issue. It's been easy for the uninformed and the apathetic to get alarmed by the claims of a small but noisy group that has resisted fluoridation over the years. Even today, fluoridation's political progress is slowed by emotional opposition.

Paragraphs 9–10 give personal comments regarding the proposition.

I am truly concerned about what is in fact a matter of national shame: that about half the children who could benefit from fluoridation are denied it. As long as adults remain indecisive about the issues, children will grow up with an accumulation of dental problems to plague them throughout life. Yet the preventive benefits of fluoridation are available at little cost.

I urge you as parents to make every effort to gain fluoridation for your children if the community you live in does not yet have it. Demand that your city officials and your state legislators take action—now.

2
The Sentence

As human beings we communicate with each other through patterns of speech called sentences, although we do not always use what is traditionally called the complete sentence. Naturally, most of us speak much more easily than we write, mainly because we have had a great deal more experience with speech than with the written word. Almost anyone, however, can improve his writing skills if he studies generally accepted principles of writing and if he practices writing according to these principles.

As an aid to improving writing, this chapter will discuss the sentence as the basic element of the English language and will show the basic sentence patterns used in the English language.

BASIC SENTENCE PATTERNS

The key to the English sentence is *word order*. If you read or heard, "Mary the dress bought," you would think that you had mis-read or had heard incorrectly. The expected order for this group of words is "Mary bought the dress." Using this expected word order, we will examine the essence of structure and meaning in English sentences.

Through study and analysis of many sentences, linguists (language experts) have recognized that words generally are arranged in one of several orders, and they have classified these arrangements as *sentence patterns*. In making these classifications, linguists did not agree on any set number of possible sentence patterns, nor did they identify a single pattern in the same way. This chapter discusses seven basic sentence patterns, used by almost all speakers of English.

Pattern 1: Subject + Verb
Pattern 2: Subject + Verb + Direct Object

Pattern 3: Subject + Verb + Direct Object + Objective Complement
Pattern 4: Subject + Verb + Indirect Object + Direct Object
Pattern 5: Subject + Verb (Linking) + Subjective Complement
Pattern 6: Subject + Form of "be" as Verb + Verb Modifier
Pattern 7: Subject + Form of "be" as Verb + Subjective Complement

Notice that sentences containing a form of "be" as the verb are in individual patterns. Forms of "be" are unlike all other verbs and therefore must be treated separately.

Each of these seven basic patterns can be expanded by adding adjective and adverb modifiers in the form of words, phrases, or clauses; compounding; adding appositives; and any combination of adding modifiers, compounding, and adding appositives. (Check the Glossary for explanation of terms that may not be familiar.)

Sentence elements in the examples will be identified as follows: subject, S; verb, V; direct object, DO; objective complement, OC; indirect object, IO; modifier, M; subjective complement, SC; appositive, A; verb modifier, VM. Phrases and clauses will also be labeled; for example, (Gerund phrase) and (Prepositional phrase). (For further discussion of gerunds and prepositions, see Chapter 7.)

Pattern 1: Subject + Verb

Pattern 1 requires two basic units: a unit to function as a subject (identifies who or what is acting in some way) and a unit to function as a verb (identifies the action done by the who or what of the subject).

    S   V
Airplanes fly.

 (Gerund phrase)
    S   V
Writing letters must suffice.

    (Clause)
    S   V
Whoever is at home should answer.

Pattern 1 may be expanded by adding modifiers. The basic pattern, however, remains unchanged; it must contain a subject and a verb.

M   S   V   M
Jet planes fly *swiftly*.

  (Gerund phrase)   (Prepositional phrase)   (Clause)
     S   M   V   M   M
Writing letters *to friends* suffices *somewhat when visits are not possible.*

Pattern 1 may also be expanded by compounding either or both of the essential units.

S   S   V
Airplanes and *gliders* fly.   (Subject compounded)

S   S   V   V
Airplanes and *gliders fly* and *soar.*   (Subject and verb compounded)

Another method of expanding Pattern 1 is by adding appositives (words added to nouns or pronouns to explain them or to give other names for them).

S   A
Airplanes, *a chief ally of the modern businessman,*

      (Prepositional phrase)
V   M
fly to all parts of the world.

S   A   V   M
Jane, *my sister,* sings well.

In addition, Pattern 1 may be expanded by any combination of adding modifiers, compounding, and adding appositives.

  (Gerund phrase)   (Gerund phrase)   (Prepositional phrase)
     S   S   M
Writing letters and making telephone calls *to friends*

(Clause)
V   M   M

suffice somewhat *when visits are not possible* but

(Clause)
M

the heart grows lonely.

(Clause)
S   A   V   M

Whoever is at home, *parent or child,* should answer immediately.

Pattern 2: Subject + Verb + Direct Object

Pattern 2 requires three basic units: a unit to function as a subject, a unit to function as a verb, and a third unit following the verb to function as a direct object (word, phrase, or clause which identifies the receiver of the action of the verb).

S   V   DO

Experiments can illustrate *theories.*

(Infinitive phrase)
S   V   DO

The team began *to play.*

(Clause)
S   V   DO

We know *that the atom can be split.*

To determine if the word, phrase, or clause following the verb is a direct object, read the subject and the verb of the sentence and add "What?" or "Whom?" to form a question. If the unit following the verb answers the question, but does not rename or describe the subject, it is the direct object.

S   V   DO

Good drivers can prevent accidents.

> Question: Good drivers can prevent what?
> Answer: "accidents" (the direct object)

S V   DO

You ask the director.

> Question: You ask whom?
> Answer: "the director" (direct object)

Pattern 2 may be expanded by the same methods illustrated in Pattern 1.

Pattern 3:   Subject + Verb + Direct Object + Objective Complement

Pattern 3 requires four basic units: a unit to function as a subject, a unit to function as a verb, a unit following the verb to function as a direct object (identifies the receiver of the action), and a unit (word or phrase) following the direct object to function as an objective complement (tells more information about the direct object by renaming or describing it).

       S   V   DO   OC

The men chose him *supervisor*.   (Objective complement renames direct object.)

       S   V   DO   OC

Practice makes the player *accurate*.   (Objective complement describes direct object.)

Pattern 3 may be expanded by the same methods illustrated in Pattern 1.

Pattern 4:   Subject + Verb + Indirect Object + Direct Object

Pattern 4 requires four basic units: a unit to function as a subject, a unit to function as a verb, a unit to function as an indirect object (specifies what or who receives the direct object), and a fourth unit to function as a direct object.

       S   V   IO   DO

The instructor gave the *students* their assignments.

       S   V   IO   DO

The salesman has taken the *customer* the furniture.

(Notice that a sentence pattern that includes an indirect object must include a direct object.)

A test of this pattern is to read the subject and the verb followed by "Whom?" and "What?" For example, the salesman has taken whom what? The answer to "Whom?" is "customer," the indirect object; the answer to "What?" is "furniture," the direct object.

If these sentences were rewritten as follows, they would be changed to Pattern 2: Subject + Verb + Direct Object. Notice that the indirect object becomes a prepositional phrase.

                                         (Prepositional phrase)

    S   V   DO   M

The instructor gave the assignments *to the students*.

                                           (Prepositional phrase)

    S   V   DO   M

The salesman has taken the furniture *to the customer*.

Pattern 4 may be expanded by the same methods illustrated in Pattern 1.

Pattern 5: Subject + Verb (Linking) + Subjective Complement

Pattern 5 requires three basic units. The first unit functions as the subject, which names who or what is being described or identified more specifically (renamed). The second unit functions as a linking verb, a verb that "links" or "joins" the subject to the subjective complement. The third unit functions as a subjective complement, a unit that tells something about the subject by describing it (sometimes identified as a predicate adjective) or renaming it (sometimes identified as a predicate nominative, a predicate noun, or a predicate pronoun).

        S   V   SC (Describes subject)

The candy tastes *good*.

        S   V   SC (Renames subject)

Father became a *dentist*.

Common linking verbs are *appear, become, feel, grow, look, remain, seem, smell, sound, taste*. A modifier following a linking verb is an adjective, not an adverb.

    Right: The rose smells sweet.
    Wrong: The rose smells sweetly.

Pattern 5 may be expanded by the same methods illustrated in Pattern 1.

Pattern 6:   Subject + Form of "be" as Verb + Verb Modifier

Pattern 6 requires three basic units: a unit to function as a subject (identifies the noun that is tied to the verb), a unit to function as a verb (a form of "be": am, is, are, was, were, be, being, been), and a third unit following the verb to function as a modifier of the verb (word, phrase, or clause which indicates location or time).

S   V   VM   (location)
The kitchen is *downstairs*.

(Prepositional phrase: time)
S   V   VM
The party will be *after the ball game*.

Pattern 6 may be expanded by the same methods illustrated in Pattern 1.

Pattern 7:   Subject + Form of "be" as Verb + Subjective Complement

Pattern 7 requires three basic units. The first unit functions as the subject, which names who or what is being described or identified more specifically (renamed). The second unit functions as a verb (a form of "be": am, is, are, was, were, be, being, been). The third unit functions as a subjective complement, a unit that tells something about the subject by describing it (sometimes identified as a predicate adjective) or renaming it (sometimes identified as a predicate nominative, a predicate noun, or a predicate pronoun).

S   V   SC (Describes subject)
They were *early*.

S   V   SC (Renames subject)
He has been a *sailor*.

Pattern 7 may be expanded by the same methods illustrated in Pattern 1.

BUILDING SENTENCES

In speaking, few of us stop and plan how we will structure our sentences. The sentences just come out because, somewhere within us, they are inexplicably put together and generated through speech.

In writing, on the other hand, the process of structuring sentences is more difficult. More often than not, we deliberately plan how to write certain sentences, and for some people this process is difficult. It will not be once you realize how sentences are constructed.

Basic Sentence Units

In the preceding section on the basic patterns that sentences form, you saw that every sentence must have two basic units: a unit to function as the subject of the sentence (identifies who or what is acting or being identified in some way) and a unit to function as the verb (identifies the assertion or the action done by the subject). Every English sentence, from the simplest to the most complicated, may be divided into two units: the subject and the verb. You also saw that the natural arrangement of these two units is subject followed by verb.

The sentence may be one word, "Wait." Its two parts are:

> S   V
> [You] Wait.   (The subject "you" is understood.)

Or it may be as complicated as:

> Unless you, your family, and friends agree to these conditions,
> S   V
> you must wait until the next session before a final judgment can be made official.

Sometimes you must rearrange the sentence into its natural order (S + V) to make this division clear.

> Has the student been instructed to register on Tuesday, not Wednesday?   (Inverted order)
> The student has been instructed to register on Tuesday, not Wednesday.   (Natural order)

To the subject and verb you can add direct objects, indirect objects and direct objects, direct objects and objective complements, subjective complements, and verb modifiers; each of these then becomes a unit of a basic sentence pattern.

Expanding the Sentence

The principal methods of expanding sentences are adding modifiers, compounding, adding appositives, and any combination of these.

ADDING MODIFIERS

A simple technique for sentence expansion is adding modifiers: words, phrases, or clauses which function as adjectives or adverbs. The sentence keeps its basic pattern (S+V, S+V+DO, S+V+DO +OC, etc.) but takes on added meaning through the adjective and/ or adverb units.

Adjective Modifiers (AdjM).   The adjective modifier may be a word, phrase, or clause, and will always modify words we call nouns or pronouns.

The machine broke.   (Basic Sentence)

Sentence expanded by adjective modifiers:

(Word)
AdjM
The *old* machine broke.

(Prepositional phrase)
AdjM
The machine *in the laboratory* broke.

(Participial phrase)
AdjM
The machine *used in Lab 141* broke.

(Infinitive phrase)
AdjM
The machine *to be used in the laboratory demonstration* broke.

(Clause)
AdjM
The machine *that was most recently assembled* broke.

Notice that every adjective modifier in the preceding examples tells which machine. The adjective modifier, whether word, phrase, or clause, answers one of three questions: Which? What kind of? How many? Study the sentences below.

(Word)
AdjM

The broken chair was repaired.   (Which chair? The broken chair.)

(Prepositional phrase)
AdjM

The organization has already received *from forty to fifty* orders.
(How many orders? From forty to fifty orders.)

(Clause)
AdjM

A horse *that lives to be thirty years old* is indeed a rarity.
(What kind of horse? A horse that lives to be thirty years old.)

Adjective modifiers most often come just before or just after the word modified.

Adverb Modifiers (AdvM). The adverb modifier may also be a word, a phrase, or a clause, but it modifies a verb, an adjective, or another adverb. Although the adverb modifier may be moved to almost any point within the sentence, the adjective· modifier generally can be placed only before or after (usually before) the word it relates to.

AdjM AdjM   AdjM
Helium is a very *light, inert,* and *colorless* gas.
(Adjective modifiers before "gas")

AdjM AdjM   AdjM
Helium is a gas, *light, inert,* and *colorless.*
(Adjective modifiers after "gas")

Now look at examples which show the movability of the adverb modifier.

AdvM
Initially, the project seemed worthless.

AdvM
The project, *initially,* seemed worthless.

AdvM
The project seemed, *initially,* worthless.

AdvM
The project seemed worthless, *initially*.

Notice that this one-word adverb "initially' may be placed at the beginning of the sentence, before the verb, after the verb, or at the end of the sentence. These are common adverb positions within the sentence.

Adverb modifiers (words, phrases, or clauses) answer such questions as *When?* (time), *Where?* (place), *Why?* (reason), *How?* (manner), *How often?* (frequency), *How much?* (amount).

AdvM
He left *quickly*.   (Answers How?)

(Phrase)   (Clause)
AdvM   AdvM
In the sixth and fifth centuries B.C., when Greeks began to ask and to try to answer certain questions, Western philosophy was born.   (Phrase and clause answer When?)

Compounding

To expand a sentence by compounding, you double a sentence unit (word, phrase, or clause), a complete sentence pattern, or both. Compounding usually requires a coordinating conjunction (and, so, for, but, or, nor, yet, both . . . and, not only . . . but also, either . . . or, neither . . . nor). This conjunction joins, links, or connects units of the same value, such as two or more subjects, two or more adjective clauses, two or more prepositional phrases, two or more sentences. The most commonly used coordinating conjunction is *and*.

S   S
Historians *and* philosophers have long recognized the importance of imaginative literature.   (Compound subject)

V   V   V
A stronger dye will *both* weaken the fabric *and* change the shade.   (Compound verb)

(Phrase)   (Phrase)   (Phrase)
Apprehending a suspect, taking him into custody, *and* questioning him, the police officer must be careful to inform the suspect of his rights.   (Compound participial phrase)

(Sentence)
Dumping garbage out to sea is an economical means of dis-
(Sentence)
posal, *but* in many instances other factors outweigh the advantages.   (Compound sentence)

ADDING APPOSITIVES

Basic sentence patterns may also be expanded by adding appositives (words, phrases, or clauses added usually to nouns or pronouns to explain them or to give another name for them). Appositives introduced by such words as "or" or "that is" may be added to
any part of speech.

A
Rubella, *or German measles,* can be controlled.   (Word in
apposition with subject)

A
We reached our goal, *to win the district championship.*
(Infinitive phrase in apposition with direct object)

A
The belief, *that the fight against cancer can be won,* is shared
by many medical researchers.   (Clause in apposition with
subject)

A
He was remunerated, that is, *paid,* for his services.   (Word
in apposition with verb)

(Notice that appositives are usually set off with commas.)

COMBINATION OF MODIFIERS, COMPOUNDS AND APPOSITIVES

Frequently, basic sentence patterns are expanded by a combination of adding modifiers, compounding, and adding appositives.

    S   A
John Quincy Adams, *sixth President of the United States,*
   V   AdvM   AdvM V
dedicated his adult life *to public service* and *finally* won the
        AdjM   AdvM
respect *of the entire nation through his honesty and devotion.*
(Combination of modifiers, compounding, and appositives)

A   S   V   AdjM

An oblong mass of rock, the Acropolis looks very much *like*

(Participial phrase)
AdjM

*a pedestal, rising abruptly about 500 feet above the city of
Athens.*   (Combination of modifiers and appositives)

EMPHASIS IN SENTENCES

In sentence construction, important parts of the sentence should stand out and less important parts should be subordinate. In the English sentence, word order controls emphasis.

1. Put material to be emphasized either at the beginning or at the end of the sentence.

> The *telephone* is a common means of communication in the twentieth century. A common means of communication in the twentieth century is the *telephone.* In the twentieth century a common means of communication is the *telephone.*

2. Emphasize important details by putting them in independent clauses and subordinate the less important details in dependent clauses and in phrases.

> Honolulu, *which is the capital of Hawaii,* is the cultural and business center of Polynesia. (Dependent clause)

> *Note:*   A dependent clause or a phrase which gives additional information not essential to the basic sentence meaning is set off by commas.

> Medieval history, *the middle period between ancient and modern history,* began with the disintegration of the Roman Empire. (Phrase used as appositive)

> *Having completed all requirements for a degree,* you may register for graduation. (Participial phrase)

3. Invert the normal order of the sentence to gain emphasis.

> SC   V   S
>
> *Unexpected* was the reaction to the new rules.

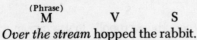

(Phrase)
M   V   S
Over the stream hopped the rabbit.

4.   Add emphasis by placing an adjective after the noun it modifies instead of before the noun.

S   AdjM   V
The professor, *tired and hungry*, listened to the final report.

S   AdjM
The opening, *tiny and mysterious*, puzzled us.

5.   Add emphasis by using verbs in the active voice. (A verb in the active voice always has a direct object.)

S   V   DO
Our team won the swimming match.

S   V   DO
Tom made the highest grade in his math class.

Using active-voice verbs strengthens emphasis because the subject *performs* the action of the verb. However, passive-voice verbs (here the subject *receives* the action of the verb) sometimes may be used for different emphasis. (The passive verb includes a form of "be" plus the past participle of the main verb.)

(1)   When the who or what is not as significant as the action or the result, passive voice may be used.

S   V
Three people were killed in the accident.

(2)   When the who or what is unknown, preferably unnamed, or relatively insignificant, passive voice may be used.

S   V
The blood sugar test was made yesterday.

S   V
The operation was performed successfully.

COMBINING IDEAS

The preceding pages have illustrated how adjective modifiers, adverb modifiers, compounding, and appositives allow you to expand sentence meaning. These techiques also offer you other advantages; you can economize on words and, at the same time, clarify word relationships. For example, the two sentences

1. Mr. Jones built a patio.
2. It is made of brick.

could be written as a single sentence

1. Mr. Jones built a brick patio.

Combining the two sentences eliminates "It is made of" and places the adjective modifier *brick* directly before the noun *patio*; thus, the relationship between the two words is clearer.

The three sentences
1. Aeschylus was the founder of Greek tragedy.
2. He was born in 525 B.C.
3. He died in 456 B.C.

could also be written as a single sentence

1. Aeschylus, who lived from 525 to 456 B.C., was the founder of Greek tragedy.

The two sentences concerning Aeschylus' life span have been combined into one dependent clause.

The ideas in sentences may be combined by adding a subordinate conjunction or a coordinate conjunction, to show the relationship between the ideas.

From the two sentences
1. The company hired him.
2. He was qualified.

a single sentence

1. The company hired him because he was qualified.

makes the relationship of ideas clearer with the addition of the subordinate conjunction "because." The second sentence changes to an adverb clause, "because he was qualified," telling why the company hired him.

The two sentences
1. John practiced every day.
2. He did not win the contest.

might be stated more clearly as

1. John practiced every day, but he did not win the contest.

The addition of the coordinate conjunction "but" indicates that the idea following it contrasts with the idea preceding it.

Study the following examples.
1. Astrology was a recognized profession.
2. It flourished until the Renaissance.
3. The new scientific discoveries of the sixteenth and seventeenth centuries ended astrology's prestige.

The ideas in these three sentences might be combined into a single sentence

1. Astrology, a recognized profession, flourished until the Renaissance; however, the new scientific discoveries of the sixteenth and seventeenth centuries ended astrology's prestige.

The addition of the conjunctive adverb "however" indicates the contrasting relationship between the two main ideas; sentences 1 and 2 have been combined into one clause.

The three sentences might also be combined as follows:
1. Although new scientific discoveries of the sixteenth and seventeenth centuries ended its prestige, astrology was a recognized profession and flourished until the Renaissance.

Almost any group of ideas can be combined in several ways. You must choose the arrangement of ideas that best "fits in with" preceding and following sentences and gives appropriate emphasis.

By using all four techniques (adjective modifiers, adverb modifiers, compounding, and appositives), you may combine the following ideas into a single sentence.

1. The mission's most important decision came.

2.   It was early on December 24.

3.   Apollo was approaching the moon.

4.   Should the spacecraft simply circle the moon and head back toward earth?

5.   Should it fire the Service Propulsion System engine and place the craft in orbit?

Ideas combined:

1.   Early on December 24, as Apollo was approaching the moon, the mission's most important decision came: should the spacecraft simply circle the moon and head back toward earth or should it fire the Service Propulsion System engine and place the craft in orbit?

Ideas also combine effectively into two or more sentences. Read the following five sentences.

1.   More than 90 percent of the electrical energy generated today is generated as alternating current rather than direct current.

2.   There are several reasons for generating energy as alternating current.

3.   Alternating current may be generated in large quantities more cheaply than direct current.

4.   Alternating current may be generated and transmitted at high voltages.

5.   These high voltages can be reduced efficiently at the receiving end of the transmission line, with small loss, to voltages suitable for lights or motors.

These five sentences combine into three.

1.   More than 90 percent of the electrical energy generated today is generated as alternating current rather than direct current.

2.   One reason is that alternating current can be generated in large quantities more cheaply.

3.   It may be generated and transmitted at high voltages that can be reduced efficiently at the receiving end of the transmission line, with small loss, to voltages suitable for lights or motors.

Sentences are used generally in groups to form paragraphs or themes. The following chapters (Chapter 3 "The Paragraph" and Chapter 4 "The Theme") discuss the planning and writing of paragraphs and themes.

3
The
Paragraph

The paragraph helps you organize material in small units and thus convey meaning more efficiently. It enables you to introduce a subject and supply sentences to support that subject through illustration, comparison, contrast, etc., as you develop the topic statement (the central idea of the paragraph).

Every kind of writing—exposition, narration, description, and argument—builds basically through paragraphs.

PLANNING THE PARAGRAPH

Before any writer puts pen or pencil to paper, he should do some thinking and planning. Just as a contractor needs a blueprint before he begins construction or a coach a plan before he and his team begin a game, a writer, whether experienced or inexperienced, needs a plan before he begins to write. This plan includes selecting a subject, limiting the subject, stating a topic sentence, adding details, and deciding on movement, transition, order, and method of development.

Selecting a Subject

The first step in planning a paragraph is to select a subject. If an instructor assigns a subject, you may bypass this step: if not, you must make this decision. You choose a topic that interests you, that you know something about, and that you can tell about in some detail. Logically, a student planning a future in engineering is interested in engineering and related fields, has some knowledge about the field, and could tell about areas in the field in some detail. On the other hand, that same student might have little interest, if any, in a topic such as the construction of ladies' wigs.

Limiting the Subject

The next step in writing the paragraph is to reduce the subject to a small subdivision. Such reducing limits or restricts a subject so that it can be written about in specific, concrete details. For example, a student could not adequately cover the subject "books" in one paragraph. The subject is too broad. He could reduce books to a subdivision such as books in libraries, but this is still too broad. He then reduces the subject to the topic, systems of classifying books. An investigation of material to be covered shows that there are only two systems for classifying books. Thus, this topic can be adequately treated, for the student's purposes, in a paragraph.

The subject books, of course, could have been limited in any number of ways and in any number of steps:

> Books > Books in libraries > Library systems of classifying books.
>
> Books > Publication of books > Copyright laws > How to copyright a book.
>
> Books > Books by American writers > Books by contemporary American writers > Books by Ralph Ellison > Ellison's *Invisible Man* > Implications of the name "Trueblood" in Ellison's *Invisible Man*.

The limiting process just described illustrates one way to limit an idea—by subject. This is usually the first step; then the limiting process may be continued through limitation by attitude, time, place, or a combination of these.

Example: A *wound* should be cleansed *gently* but *thoroughly before stitches are taken.*

Almost any single-idea sentence is limited by subject and attitude. The subject identifies what will be written about and the attitude pinpoints the writer's point of view toward the subject, or how he feels about the subject.

The important thing to remember in narrowing a subject for a paragraph is that the topic finally decided upon must be so limited that it can be satisfactorily developed within *one* paragraph. (The term *satisfactorily developed* is relative, of course, depending on the purpose of the paragraph.)

The Topic Statement

In the preceding step, the subject "books" was limited to library systems of classifying books; the limited idea can now be stated in a sentence:

> Libraries classify books according to one of two systems: the Library of Congress Classification or the Dewey Decimal Classification.

This sentence is the topic statement, the central idea to be developed in the paragraph. The topic statement is sometimes expressed in a phrase within a longer sentence; more frequently, however, it appears in a main clause, with additional information (as in the illustrative paragraph on page 52 about airplanes). But most often—and usually most effectively—the topic statement is a short, simple sentence.

Every topic statement has key words or phrases that tell the writer exactly what he must include in developing the paragraph. For example, in the topic statement, "Libraries classify books according to one of two systems: the Library of Congress Classification or the Dewey Decimal Classification," the key words are *libraries* and *two systems. Libraries*, as the subject of the sentence, identifies the topic; the comment made in the remainder of the sentence tells what about *libraries* will be discussed. The paragraph developing the topic statement will not be about *libraries;* rather it will be about the *two systems libraries use to classify books*.

Everything in the paragraph must discuss the Library of Congress Classification and the Dewey Decimal Classification as the two ways in which libraries classify books. The writer could not discuss how to check out a book or the arrangement of books in his personal library because these subjects are not introduced by the topic statement and the key words within the topic statement.

POSITION OF THE TOPIC SENTENCE

Although the topic statement may be placed at several different positions in a paragraph, most often it appears at the beginning. As the writer develops the paragraph, frequent rereading of the topic sentence will help him stick to his limited topic and avoid wandering into a discussion of related ideas that have no place within the paragraph being developed. The paragraph must include only material related to the central idea given in the topic statement. In the following paragraph, the central idea is in the opening sentence.

> *Topic statement first. What makes an airplane fly is air—*not the engine, the propeller, the pilot, or some gadget inside the cockpit. As the plane gathers speed from its engine, the curved upper surface of the wing forces the air to move faster over it than the air flowing under the straight surface beneath. Thus, the air on top becomes thinner, has less pressure, and the denser air beneath the wing exerts more pressure, creating "lift." Of course the power of the engine, the overall design of the plane, weight, temperature, altitude, and other factors aid the mastery over gravity and air space. However, it is the perfected design of streamlined "airfoil" moving at high speeds that keeps the airplane flying. Shape any material like an airplane and toss it into the air. It will fly, proving that air, with the impact of the shape on the air, keeps the plane aloft and flying.

The skillful writer often moves the topic statement from the beginning to other positions within the paragraph. For example, he might place the topic statement at the end of the paragraph.

> *Topic statement last.* The bones of dogs have been found in numerous campsites of the New Stone Age, dating back more than 10,000 years. The domestication of dogs, then, probably began many thousands of years earlier than that. From these campsite remains, at least five different kinds of dogs comparable to modern dogs have been identified. *Thus, one can assume that the dog, undoubtedly used in hunting, was one of the first animals domesticated by man.*

Sometimes the skillful writer might omit the topic statement and imply rather than state the main idea. However, having read a paragraph with an implied topic statement, the reader should be able to state, without doubt, the topic statement developed. The following paragraph has no stated topic statement, yet a reader knows immediately upon reading it that the topic developed is a historical description of the legendary serpent, the basilisk.

> *Topic statement implied.* The basilisk was described by Pliny the Elder, in the first century, as a snake with a small golden crown. By the Middle Ages, however, it had become a snake with the head of a cock or of a human being. The basilisk, or cockatrice as it came to be known, was born of a spherical egg laid by a seven-year-old cock during the dog days of summer. The egg was then hatched by a toad. The basilisk was so horrible and dreadful in appearance that mere sight of it was fatal. The only way to kill the creature was to make it look at its own reflection in a mirror.

The beginning and the ending of a paragraph are common positions for the topic statement, but it is not unusual to find a topic statement implied.

Details

Once a subject has been limited and the central idea stated in a topic statement, the next step is to think of possible details that might develop the topic statements. Details *support* general statements and help make them more specific.

ADDING DETAILS

It is quite helpful to jot down on scratch paper possible supporting details and then select the ones to include in the paragraph and eliminate the others.

In thinking of possible details, consider what the topic sentence asks for. The key words in the topic sentence, "Libraries classify books according to one of two systems: the Library of Congress Classification or the Dewey Decimal Classification," give clues to possible details for supporting the idea.

Here is a topic sentence with a list of possible supporting details.

Topic sentence: Libraries classify books according to one of two systems: the Library of Congress Classification or the Dewey Decimal Classification.

Possible details: 1.   Library of Congress (LC) system has 20 basic groups.
2.   List of basic groups of LC.

3. Dewey Decimal Classification (DD) has 10 basic groups.
4. List of basic DD groups.
5. Reasons a library chooses one system over another.
6. LC uses letters and numbers.
7. LC letters and numbers used to form many subdivisions.
8. Origin of the LC system.
9. Origin of the DD system: Melvil Dewey thought of the idea while sitting in church.
10. DD uses numbers.
11. The DD numbers are divided to form many subdivisions.
12. Most libraries use the DD system.
13. Smaller libraries use the DD.
14. In LC, six unused letters—for future classifications.
15. Book *Lasers and Their Applications* in LC: TK7872.L3S7.
16. Same book in DD: 621.329.
17. Subdivisions in DD designated by numeral-decimal combination.

Once all details that come to mind are jotted down, analyze the topic sentence carefully to be sure which details can best be used to develop the main idea. Then carefully consider the list of details, modifying and combining where necessary, and eliminate those that do not seem valuable.

Checking the preceding list might eliminate the details crossed out below.

Topic sentence: Libraries classify books according to one of two systems: the Library of Congress Classification or the Dewey Decimal Classification.

Possible details: 1. Library of Congress (LC) system has 20 basic groups.
2. Listing of basic groups of LC.

3. Dewey Decimal Classification (DD) has 10 basic groups.
4. ~~List of basic DD groups.~~
5. ~~Reasons a library chooses one system over another.~~
6. LC uses letters and numbers.
7. LC letters and numbers used to form many subdivisions.
8. ~~Origin of the LC system.~~
9. ~~Origin of the DD system: Melvil Dewey thought of the idea while sitting in church.~~
10. DD uses numbers.
11. The DD numbers are divided to form many subdivisions.
12. Most libraries use the DD system.
13. Smaller libraries use the DD.
14. In LC, six unused letters—for future classifications.
15. Book *Lasers and Their Applications* in LC: TK7872.L3S7.
16. Same book in DD: 621.329.
17. Subdivisions in DD designated by numeral-decimal combination.

These remaining details can be combined to develop a satisfactory paragraph.

DEVELOPING THE PARAGRAPH

Movement, Transition, Order and Method of Development

Now you are ready to plan how to put topic sentence and details together. At this point in planning, consider at least four points: movement, transition, order, and method (pattern) of development.

MOVEMENT

Movement within the paragraph may be either sequential or expanding.

Sequential Movement. The details in a paragraph may be so arranged that the movement is a sequence, a progression of thought, a moving forward, a series of actions. A paragraph of "First you do this," "Second you do this," etc. is sequential in its movement. Read the following paragraph explaining how an allergy develops, and note that the movement within it is sequential.

Different allergies develop in a similar way. First, an individual must be particularly susceptible to a specific substance, or allergen. When he initially comes in contact with this allergen, his body produces antibodies as protection against it. But the next time he comes in contact with this same allergen, the antibodies that have been developed in the blood stream react against the allergen. In this reaction a chemical substance, histamine, is released from the tissues, causing a series of other reactions that result in inflamed and running eyes and nose, swelling, itching, and similar discomforts.

Expanding Movement.   Movement in a paragraph may add one idea to another so that the paragraph does not really progress; it expands, or builds. A paragraph defining a term would have such movement; "This term means . . .," "It also means . . .," etc. A paragraph discussing advantages or disadvantages of an object or a system would also expand as it develops. The following descriptive paragraph develops expansively by stacking one detail on top of another.

The Picton boat was due to leave at half-past eleven. It was a beautiful night, mild, starry; only when they got out of the cab and started to walk down the Old Wharf that jutted out into the harbor, a faint wind blowing off the water ruffled under Fenella's hat, and she had to put up a hand to keep it on. It was dark on the Old Wharf, very dark; the wool sheds, the cattle trucks, the cranes standing up so high, the little squat railway engine, all seemed carved out of solid darkness. Here and there on a rounded woodpile, that was like the stalk of a huge black mushroom, there hung a lantern, but it seemed afraid to unfurl its timid, quivering light in all that blackness; it burned softly, as if for itself. *

TRANSITION

Transition in a paragraph relates one thought to another so that there is a clear, coherent progression between them. In speaking we can show such relationships by frowning, stomping a foot,

*From "The Voyage" by Katherine Mansfield.

or shaking a finger or even a fist if the occasion calls for stronger emphasis. In writing the paragraph we must use words, and our language has an ample supply of such words, usually grouped under the identifying term *transitional words and phrases. Transition* refers to a word, phrase, sentence, or even a group of sentences that relate a preceding thought or topic to a succeeding thought or topic.

Transition through Conjunction. Conjunctions are familiar transitional words. To show that several items are of equal value, we use the word "and."

Item 1, item 2, item 3, *and* item 4

"And," of course, is the conjunction that means "also," or "in addition," and it indicates the relationship of sameness or similarity between ideas.

To show difference or contrast between items, we would use "but."

Other conjunctions and the relationships they show include:

for (condition)   or (choice)
nor (exclusion)   yet (condition)

Transition through Conventional Phrases.   Another large group of transitional words and phrases that show relationships between items includes such terms as the following:

accordingly	no doubt
as a result	often
at the same time	once
by contrast	on the other hand
consequently	similarly
finally	specifically
first	thus
for example	to be sure
frequently	to conclude
in addition	to sum up
in general	usually
in other words	

Transition through Other Techniques.   Other techniques to ensure a smooth flow of sentences and thoughts are pronoun reference, repetition of key terms, continuity of sentence subjects, parallel sentence patterns, or a combination of these. In the following paragraph from Abraham Lincoln's Gettysburg Address, italics have been added to indicate these transition techniques.

Continuity of subject "we":
Repetition of key terms
  "war," "nation," and
  "battlefield":
Parallel sentence patterns:

Pronoun reference:

Now *we* are engaged in a great civil *war*, testing whether that *nation* or any other *nation* so conceived and so dedicated, can long endure. *We* are met on a great *battlefield* of that *war*. *We* have come to dedicate a portion of *that field*, as a final resting place for those who *here* gave their lives that that *nation* might live. It is altogether fitting and proper that *we* should do *this*.

    Transition and Continuity.   Read the following paragraph.

    Milling of copper begins in a concentrator. Crushed ore must be ground into fine particles. Water and the crushed ore make a soupy mixture. Milling of copper requires ball mills. Small particles come out and pass through a screen with 10,000 openings to the square inch. A flotation process concentrates the particles. There are containers called flotation cells. Chemicals and oil are added. Paddles or air jets agitate to make it bubble. The chemicals affect it. Bubbles and mineral particles make a froth. After being scraped off and dried, this is called concentrate.

Although the preceding paragraph contains information, it is difficult to understand because there are no transitional words and phrases, or any other techniques, to relate one idea to another. Read the same paragraph revised.

    The milling of copper begins in a concentrator. First water is added to crushed ore to form a soup-like mixture called slurry. The slurry passes into ball mills containing cylinders. As the cylinders rotate, the balls grind the ore into particles small enough to pass through a screen with 10,000 openings to the square inch. The slurry next goes through a flotation process that concentrates the mineral-bearing particles. In the flotation process the slurry passes into containers called flotation cells. There chemicals and oil are added, and the entire mixture is agitated by paddles or air jets to make it bubble. One chemical makes the bubble stable; another chemical coats the mineral particles so that they stick to the bubbles. The bubbles with the mineral particles rise to the top of the cell and form a froth. Finally, this froth is scraped off and dried. What remains is copper concentrate that may contain from 15 to 33 percent copper.

Now, study the methods by which transition, or continuity, is achieved in the paragraph, as indicated in the explanatory notes. (In the notes s. = sentence.)

Key word "copper" repeated in s. 11:

(1) The milling of *copper* begins in a concentrator. (2) *First* water is added

Transitional marker "First" indicates a step in the milling process:

Key word "ore," repeated in s. 4, refers to copper in s. 1:

to crushed *ore* to form a soup-like *mix-*

"Mixture" and "slurry" synonyms; similar association in s. 7:

ture called *slurry.* (3) The *slurry* passes

Key word "slurry" repeated as subject of s. 3, 5, 6:

Repetition of "ball" and "cylinders" ties s. 4 to s. 5:

into *ball* mills containing *cylinders.* (4) As the *cylinders* rotate, the *balls* grind the *ore* into *particles* small enough to pass through a screen with 10,000 openings to the square inch.

Key word "particles" gains importance when modified to "mineral particles" in s. 5, 8, and 9:

Transitional marker "next" indicates a step in the milling process:

(5) The *slurry next* goes through a

Repetition of "flotation process" ties s. 5 to s. 6:

flotation process that concentrates the *mineral-bearing particles.* (6) In the *flotation process* the slurry passes into containers called *flotation cells.* (7) *There* chemicals and oil are added, and the entire *mixture* is agitated by

Repetition of "flotation" connects "flotation cells" with "flotation process" in s. 5 and 6; "cell" in s. 9 refers to "flotation cells":

"There" repeats meaning of "containers called flotation cells":

Pronoun "it" refers to "mix-ture":

Key word "bubble" repeated in s. 8 and 9:

Contrast of "one chemical" in first half of sentence with "another chemical" in second half:

Pronoun "they" refers to "mineral particles":

Repetition of "froth" ties s. 9 to s. 10:

Transitional marker "Finally" indicates last step in the milling process:

paddles or air jets to make *it bubble.*

(8) *One chemical* makes the *bubble* stable; *another chemical* coats the

mineral particles so that *they* stick to the *bubbles.* (9) The *bubbles* with the *mineral particles* rise to the top of the cell and form a *froth.* (10) *Finally, this froth* is scraped off and dried. (11) What remains is *copper* concentrate that may contain from 15 to 33 percent *copper.*

ORDER

Movement and transition in the paragraph relate closely to the order or arrangement of details. Some common orders are time order, space order, general to particular, particular to general, and climax. You must decide what order best arranges your selected details.

Time order. In a paragraph using time, or chronological, order, arrange the events according to *when* they happened. For example, you might use time order to report your progress in completing course requirements in a major field. You could report the completed courses in the order in which they were taken. Also, in explaining a particular operation or narrating an experience, you would use time order. Study the following paragraph; in it the writer gives directions for treating a serious burn. The order is time.

> Take the following action in treating a serious burn. Remove any loose clothing on or near the burn. Cover the injury with a clean dry dressing. Being careful not to touch the dressing, wash the area around the burn. Then, with tape or bandage, secure the dressing in place tightly enough to keep out air. If fingers or toes or other adjoining skin areas are burned, separate them with gauze or cloth to prevent their sticking together. Unless recommended by a doctor, do not apply medication.

Space order. In a paragraph using spatial order, discuss the items according to *where* they are. For example, in describing the physical layout of a college, you might show certain buildings located to the south of a main building, others to the north, and still others directly to the east of the main building. Also, in describing room by room the luxurious features of a house, you would use space order. In the following paragraph, the details describing Huck Finn's father, Pap, are presented in a space order; the sequence of movement is from head to toe to floor.

> He was almost fifty, and he looked it. His hair was long and tangled and greasy, and hung down, and you could see his eyes shining through like he was behind vines. It was all black, no gray; so was his long, mixed-up whiskers. There warn't no color in his face, where his face showed; it was white; not like another man's white, but a white to make a body sick, a white to make a body's flesh crawl—a tree-toad white, a fish-belly white. As for his clothes —just rags, that was all. He had one ankle resting on 'tother knee; the boot on that foot was busted, and two of his toes stuck through, and he worked them now and then. His hat was laying on the floor; an old black slouch with the top caved in, like a lid.*

General to particular (specific) order. In a paragraph using general to particular order, the topic sentence, the most general statement within the paragraph, appears near the beginning of the paragraph. Following the topic sentence, the body of the paragraph contains details giving additional information, examples, comparisons, contrasts, reasons, etc.—the particular or the specific material of the paragraph. This is the order most often used by students and with good reason. Placing the topic sentence near the beginning of the paragraph allows you to reread the sentence often as you write your paragraph and helps you stick to the main idea stated in the topic sentence. The following paragraph illustrates general to particular order.

> Lures for bass fishing should be selected according to the time of day for fishing. For early morning and late afternoon fishing, use top-water baits that make a bubbling or splashing sound. For midday fishing, select deep-running lures and plastic worms. And for night fishing try any kind of bait that makes a lot of noise and has a lot of action. The reason for selecting these different baits is

*From *Adventures of Huckleberry Finn* by Samuel Langhorne Clemens.

that bass, in the early morning, in the late afternoon, and at night, feed on top of the shallow water; the only way to get their attention is to use a noisy, top-water lure. During the middle of the day, however, the bass swim down to cooler water; then a deep-running lure is best.

Particular (specific) to general order.   A paragraph using particular to general order reverses the general to particular order; the most general statement, or the topic sentence, is near the end of the paragraph. The specific material—reasons, examples, comparisons, details, etc.—precede and lead up to the topic sentence, as in the following paragraph.

> The human body requires energy for growth and activity; this energy is provided through calories in food. The weight of an adult is determined, in general, by the balance of the intake of energy in food with the expenditure of energy in activity and growth. When intake and outgo of energy are equal, weight will stay the same. Similarly, weight is reduced when the body receives fewer calories from food than it uses, and weight is increased when the body receives more calories than it uses. Weight can be controlled, therefore, by regulating either the amount of food eaten, or the extent of physical activity, or both.

Climax.   In a paragraph using the order of climax, arrange the ideas so that each succeeding idea is more important than the preceding. The most important idea comes as the last statement of the paragraph.

> People often drink water without knowing for sure that it is safe to drink. They drink water from driven wells into which potentially impure surface water has drained. They drink water from springs without checking around the outlet of the spring to be sure that no surface pollution from man or animal wastes has occurred. Without knowing the rate of flow, the degree of pollution, or the temperature, they drink running water, thinking it safe because of a popular notion that running water purifies itself. These are dangerous acts; polluted water can kill!

Other orders.   Among other orders of paragraph development are alphabetical and random listing, least important to most important, least pertinent to most pertinent, least likely to most likely, simple to complex, known to unknown.

METHOD OF DEVELOPMENT

Another point to be considered before writing is method or pattern of development. Some common methods are illustration or example, comparison (similarity) and contrast (differences), cause and effect (things happen and the results of their happening), definition (defining a term, a process, etc.), and analysis through partition (division into parts). More than likely any one paragraph will contain a combination of methods of development.

Examples or illustrations. A single, lengthy illustration, or several examples or illustrations, can effectively develop a topic sentence into a paragraph. The following sample paragraph includes several brief examples.

> The decade between 1920 and 1930 is often referred to as sports' golden age, primarily because of the caliber of performance of many noted competitors. In baseball, for instance, there were Ty Cobb and George Herman (Babe) Ruth, who set a major league home run record of 60 in 1927. Jack Dempsey, the heavyweight boxing champion, became well known for his quick victories. Lawn tennis supplied William T. (Big Bill) Tilden, considered by many the finest all-round player in the game's history. Golf's Robert T. (Bobby) Jones, Jr., football's "Red" Grange, swimming's Johnny Weissmuller, figure skating's Sonja Henie—all are examples from the impressive list of competitors in sports' golden 20's.

Comparison and contrast. Comparison is a method showing similarity between two or more people, ideas, or objects; and contrast is a method showing the difference or differences between two or more people, ideas, or objects.

Comparison emphasizes the similarity between apparently unlike things, especially when one is unfamiliar; through comparing the unfamiliar with the familiar, the unfamiliar becomes clearer. Contrast, on the other hand, emphasizes the difference between apparently like things.

There are two ways to arrange material for comparison and contrast. In the first way, the material consists of two parts: the first part discusses one of the two things compared; the second discusses the other, taking up the same points in the same order as discussed in the first part.

The following paragraph, which discusses differences in the moral values expressed in the fiction of Hemingway and Faulkner, uses this arrangement. The first part discusses Hemingway's emphasis on personal moral values and the second part discusses Faulkner's emphasis on social moral values. Notice the transition from the first part to the second part with the sentence, "In contrast, Faulkner's moral values are social rather than personal."

Topic sentence: Both Ernest Hemingway and William Faulkner, as exemplified in their fiction, are concerned
Part 1:   with moral values. For Hemingway the paramount virtue is courage. Man cannot be victorious in the struggles in which he is involved; therefore, the important thing is how he behaves, how he reacts. If man faces his defeat without cowardice, then he achieves "grace under pressure." This triumph of sorts gives meaning and dignity to his struggle. In contrast,
Transition: Faulkner's moral values are social rather than
Part 2:   personal. The South's curse was slavery, whose problems multiplied after the Civil War. The people of virtue, both white and black, try to solve the problems; but their attempts are often futile in face of those who are conniving and unscrupulous.

A second way to arrange material for comparison and contrast takes up separate points one by one and completes each point before going to the next. The following sample paragraph, which contrasts the alligator and the crocodile, uses this arrangement.

Topic sentence: The alligator is a close relative of the crocodile.
Point 1:   The alligator, however, has a broader head and
Point 2:   blunter snout. Alligators are usually found in
Point 3:   fresh water; crocodiles prefer salt water. The
Point 4:   alligator's lower teeth, which fit inside the edge of the upper jaw, are not visible when the lipless mouth is closed. The crocodile's teeth are always visible.

Cause and effect. A third method or pattern for arranging ideas into paragraph form is cause and effect. Using this pattern, you may move in two directions: from cause to effect, or, reversing this movement, from discussing effects first to identifying the cause. In the following paragraph, movement is from cause (passage of the Stamp Act) to effect (action of the Stamp Act congress in the American colonies).

> The passage of the Stamp Act in 1765 by the British Parliament aroused great excitement in the American colonies. Interpreting the Act as an attempt at taxation without representation, the colonies assembled a Stamp Act congress. This congress formulated an address to the king, petitions to Parliament, and a declaration of the rights and grievances of the colonies. It asserted that the colonies could be taxed only by their own representatives in the colonial assemblies, claimed the inherent right of trial by jury, and proclaimed the Stamp Act as an expression of the subversion of the rights and liberties of the colonies.

To gain suspense or to make a point dramatically, you may choose to give the effects first and then identify the cause.

> Then rose a frightful cry—the hoarse, hideous, indescribable cry of hopeless fear—the despairing animal cry man utters when suddenly brought face to face with Nothingness, without preparation, without consolation, without possibility of respite. . . . *Sauve qui peut!* Some wrenched down the doors; some clung to the heavy banquet tables, to the sofas, to the billiard tables: during one terrible instant, against fruitless heroisms, against futile generosities, raged all the frenzy of selfishness, all the brutalities of panic. And then, then came, thundering through the blackness, the giant swells, boom on boom! . . . One crash! The huge frame building rocks like a cradle, seesaws, crackles. What are human shrieks now? The tornado is shrieking! Another! Chandeliers splinter; lights are dashed out; a sweeping cataract hurls in: the immense hall rises, oscillates, twirls as upon a pivot, crepitates, crumbles into ruin. Crash again! The swirling wreck dissolves into the wallowing of another monster billow; and a hundred cottages overturn, spin in sudden eddies, quiver, disjoint, and melt into the seething. . . . So the hurricane passed.*

*From *Chita* by Lafcadio Hearn

Definition. A fourth method or pattern of paragraph development is definition. This arrangement gives details to explain the nature and characteristics of the term being defined and often begins with a sentence definition. A sentence definition names the term, states the class or group to which it belongs, and gives its essential, distinguishing characteristics. This sentence definition is then expanded in the remainder of the paragraph through such details as a description of the item, an explanation of its function, and an analysis of its parts. The following paragraph defines "adolescence."

> Adolescence is the period of physical and emotional transition when a person discards his childish ways and prepares for the duties and responsibilities of adulthood. During this period he is neither child nor adult, although he has characteristics of both. "To grow to maturity," the meaning of the derivative Latin word *adolescere*, describes the state of the adolescent. This period of transition is customarily divided into three phases: preadolescence, or puberty, the approximately two-year period of sexual maturing; early adolescence, extending from the time of sexual maturity to the age of sixteen and a half; and the late adolescence, extending from the age of sixteen and a half to twenty-one.

Analysis through partition. Analysis through partition divides a thing into parts, steps, or aspects. Each division is discussed, showing its individual function and its relationship to the whole.

> The United States government has three branches: the legislative, the executive, and the judicial. The legislative branch is responsible for enacting laws. Legislators, or Congressmen, from each state are elected by the popular vote of that state. Members of the House of Representatives have a two-year term; members of the Senate, a six-year term. The executive branch is responsible for carrying out (executing) the laws enacted by the Congress. The chief executives, the President and the Vice-President, are chosen by the Electoral College for a four-year term. The third branch of the government, the judicial, is entrusted with interpreting the laws. This branch is headed by the Supreme Court, composed of nine persons appointed for life by the President. Because of the different methods of selecting the chief members of each branch and their different lengths of term in office, each branch serves as a check and balance for the other branches.

WRITING THE PARAGRAPH

Writing the First Draft

Once the preceding steps have been completed—selecting a subject, limiting the subject, stating a topic sentence, adding details, and deciding on movement, transition, order, and method of development—you are ready to write a first draft of the paragraph. In this first writing it may be helpful to identify the selected details as *major* supporting details or as *minor* supporting details.

MAJOR AND MINOR SUPPORTING DETAILS

Major supporting details give direct support to the key idea stated in the topic sentence.

Topic sentence:	Libraries classify books according to one of two systems: the Library of Congress Classification or the Dewey Decimal Classification.
Major support 1:	The Library of Congress Classification divides all books into twenty basic groups.
Major support 2:	The Dewey Decimal Classification divides all books into ten basic groups.
Major support 3:	The designations for the book *Lasers and Their Applications* illustrate differences in the two systems.

For a more exact discussion, the major ideas supporting the topic sentence should be developed further by minor supporting details.

Topic sentence:	Libraries classify books according to one of two systems: the Library of Congress Classification or the Dewey Decimal Classification.
Major support 1:	The Library of Congress Classification divides all books into twenty basic groups.
Minor support:	Each group is indicated by a letter of the alphabet.
Minor support:	The six letters not currently used are for future classification expansion.
Minor support:	The basic groups have many divisions.

Minor support:	Subdivisions are designated by letter-number combinations.
Major support 2:	The Dewey Decimal Classification divides all books into ten basic groups.
Minor support:	Each group is indicated by a number.
Minor support:	The basic group are divided and subdivided numerous times.
Minor support:	Subdivisions are designated by numeral-decimal combinations.
Major support 3:	The designations for the book *Lasers and Their Applications* illustrate differences in the two systems.
Minor support:	The Library of Congress designation is TK7872.L3S7.
Minor support:	The Dewey Decimal designation is 621.329.

There is no required number of major or minor supporting details in any one paragraph. You might write a paragraph containing only major supports for the topic sentence or a paragraph with one major support and the remaining details minor supports. You must decide how to develop your selected topic sentence.

Further, there may be sentences in the paragraph other than the topic sentence that would not give major or minor supporting details. For example, a final sentence stating a conclusion, such as "It is not feasible to begin plant expansion at this time," gives neither major nor minor support; it simply concludes the paragraph. Sometimes the topic sentence may need a sentence or sentences explaining the central idea; this would be an explanatory sentence, not a major or a minor support. Or, a paragraph may contain transition sentences that connect major details.

Topic sentence:	Libraries classify books according to one of two systems: the Library of Congress Classification or the Dewey Decimal Classification.
Major support:	The Library of Congress Classification divides all books into twenty basic groups.
Transition sentence:	The Dewey Decimal Classification, however, the older and more common system, is the one used by most libraries, especially smaller libraries.

Major support:	The Dewey Decimal Classification divides all books into ten basic groups.

PUTTING SENTENCES TOGETHER

A first draft of a paragraph on the two library systems of classifying books might look like this.

Topic sentence:	Libraries classify books according to one of two systems: the Library of Congress Classification or the Dewey Decimal Classification.
Major support 1:	The Library of Congress Classification divides all books into twenty basic groups;
Minor support:	each group is indicated by a letter of the alphabet.
Minor support:	(The six letters not currently used are for future classification expansion.)
Minor support:	These basic groups have many divisions,
Minor support:	designated by a letter-number combination.
Transition sentence:	The Dewey Decimal Classification, however, the older and more common system, is the one used by most libraries, especially smaller libraries.
Major support 2:	The Dewey Decimal Classification divides all books into ten basic groups,
Minor support:	using a number system.
Minor support:	These basic groups are divided and then subdivided numerous times, all on the decimal (by tens) system.
Major support 3:	The book *Lasers and Their Applications* has the following designations, with each letter and each numeral having a particular significance:
Minor support:	Library of Congress TK7872.L3S7
Minor support:	Dewey Decimal 621.329

Revising

Check to see if the paragraph needs any revisions or corrections, using the following checklist for suggestions. Then make these changes before copying the paragraph a final time.

Checklist for Revising

Topic sentence
1. Carefully stated so that the main idea is evident
2. If implied, main idea evident upon reading the paragraph

Words
1. Words chosen carefully to convey exact meaning
2. Words used economically; no wordiness
3. Each word spelled correctly
4. Correct usage of words that sound alike: *to, too, two; its, it's; there, their, they're;* etc.
5. No words carelessly omitted

Sentences
1. All ideas expressed in complete sentences
2. Sentence structure varied to avoid monotony
3. No run-on sentences

Transition
1. Transitional techniques used to keep sentences moving smoothly from one to another
2. Transitional words and phrases used to show relationship between ideas

Development
1. Main idea developed by including specific details of support
2. All details clearly related to main idea

Punctuation
1. Correct comma usage
2. Correct end punctuation

Grammatical usage
1. Subject-verb agreement
2. Correct verb form
3. Correct case of pronoun

Content
1. Accurate
2. Complete

General
1. Legible writing
2. Acceptable manuscript form

Making the Final Copy

Now make a copy of the revised draft. Read the final copy carefully to catch any careless mistakes, such as in spelling or punctuation. If the paragraph has been typed, check to be sure there are no typographical errors.

> Libraries classify books according to one of two systems: the Library of Congress Classification or the Dewey Decimal Classification. The Library of Congress Classification divides all books into twenty basic groups, each group indicated by a letter of the alphabet (the six letters not currently used are for future classification expansion). These basic groups have many divisions, designated by a letter-number combination. The Dewey Decimal Classification, however, the older and more common system, is the one used by most libraries, especially smaller libraries. The Dewey Decimal Classification divides all books into ten basic groups, using a number system. These basic groups are divided and then subdivided numerous times, all on the decimal (by tens) system. As an example of the differences in the two classifying systems, the book *Lasers and Their Applications* has the following designations, with each letter and each numeral having a particular significance: Library of Congress, TK7872.L3S7; Dewey Decimal, 621.329.

PARAGRAPHS OF INTRODUCTION, TRANSITION, AND CLOSING

The preceding pages of this chapter have dealt with paragraphs that are developmental: the paragraphs may stand alone as a single unit developing an idea, or they may be in a series developing a stated topic. There are at least three other types of paragraphs—introductory, transition, and closing. Although these paragraphs may add details, they are used primarily to introduce a topic, to connect sections of a paper, or to end a paper.

Paragraph of Introduction

A very important paragraph in a long selection is the introductory paragraph. This is what the reader sees first; it could well determine whether he continues reading or puts the selection aside. The introductory paragraph should get the reader's attention and introduce the subject being discussed.

Some introductory paragraphs provide a guide for the theme to follow by *stating the major points the writer will develop* to support his topic.

> Although most people would refer to the writing employed in the English language as "English," it might also be designated "Latin," for English writing is very similar to the Latin writing of more than 2000 years ago. The development of Latin writing can be traced backward through Latin, Greek, Semitic, and Egyptian.

It is evident that the major points to be developed in paragraphs that follow will be the steps in the development of Latin writing.

The introductory paragraph may *introduce the central idea without giving any specific statements about ideas* to be used in development.

> The relatively thin upper layer of the earth's crust is called soil. One dictionary definition of *soil* is "finely divided rock material mixed with decayed vegetable or animal matter, constituting that portion of the surface of the earth in which plants grow, or may grow." This upper layer of the earth's surface, varying in thickness from six to eight inches in the case of humid soils to ten or twenty feet in the case of arid soils, possesses characteristic properties that distinguish it from the underlying rocks and rock ingredients.

A theme following this introductory paragraph would list and discuss the properties of the upper layer of the earth's surface. At this point, however, these properties have not been identified.

Paragraph of Transition

The paragraph of transition connects two paragraphs or two sets of paragraphs. Usually brief (often only one or two sentences), the transition paragraph signals a marked shift in thought between two sections of a composition. The transition paragraph looks back to the preceding paragraph, summarizes the preceding material, or indicates the material to come.

Not all compositions, of course, require transition paragraphs. Frequently a transitional word, phrase, or sentence is sufficient to connect the sections. You must decide, after considering the purpose and method of development in your theme, whether it is more effective to show transition between paragraphs through the opening and closing sentences of the adjacent paragraphs, or whether it is more effective to use a transition paragraph.

For instance, in a theme discussing the advantages and disadvantages of living at home while attending college, you might decide that you need a transition paragraph to connect the "advantages" section of the theme with the "disadvantages" section.

> Thus, the student who lives at home while attending college has fewer living expenses, he is free from dormitory rules, and he can enjoy the conveniences of family living. On the other hand, he must consider that he misses the experience of dormitory life, that he has less opportunity to meet other students, that he spends a lot of time and money commuting, and that he has less opportunity to become independent in making decisions.

The first sentence summarizes the first section of the theme; the second sentence looks forward to the next section by suggesting the material that is to come.

Paragraph of Closing

The closing paragraph, which leaves a final impression on the reader, may bring the theme to a close in several ways. A theme discussing the pros and cons of advertising might have the following closing paragraph.

> Many other good and bad points of advertising could be given. But these are sufficient to suggest the relation of advertising to people's lives, the vast power it controls, and the social responsibilities it carries.

This paragraph *draws a conclusion* about the material discussed in the theme.

A theme explaining the primary differences between plants and animals might end with the following *summary* paragraph.

> The primary differences between plants and animals, then, are these: animals can move about, animals sense their surroundings, animals live on ready-made foods, and animals do not contain cellulose.

This paragraph *reemphasizes the main points* discussed in the theme.

Remember that many short themes, three to four pages, do not need closing paragraphs. Actually there is no one rule to guide you in deciding if a closing paragraph is needed. You must read the theme through and, if it seems to end abruptly, consider adding a closing paragraph—usually either a conclusion or a summary.

4
The
Theme

The theme (essay, composition), whether exposition, narration, description, or argument, is a group of paragraphs developing a limited topic or idea. The major difference between the theme and the paragraph is that a larger amount of material is covered in the theme.

PLANNING THE THEME

The steps in planning and writing the theme are essentially the same as those followed in planning and writing the paragraph. You select a subject, limit it to an area manageable in time and length, state the central idea to be developed, select and list details to support the central idea, outline these details, develop the theme from the outline, revise, and proofread.

Selecting a Subject

When planning a theme, remember to select a subject that interests you, that you know something about, and that you can write about in some detail to communicate with an identified reader or audience. An individual knows most about himself; such subjects, therefore, as personal experiences, feelings, attitudes, and beliefs offer good possibilities. Personal experiences include trips and vacations, reading, "firsts" (first day at college, first date, first day on the job, first fishing trip), or any other experience. Feelings, attitudes toward and beliefs about any subject (education, relations between man and man, war, love, success) also offer excellent topics for writing.

Consider the time allowed to complete the theme and the length. If the time is a class period (approximately one hour), the theme will of necessity be brief (two-to-three pages); the topic selected, therefore, must be limited to a point that can be discussed in some detail in the allotted time and space.

Keep in mind that the choice of subject is less important than how you develop it. Almost any topic is satisfactory, with proper limitation, of course, but the development is the significant thing— the organization of the material, the clear relationship of ideas, the specific details selected, and the conventional usage of grammar, spelling, and punctuation.

Limiting the Subject

The next step in planning a theme is to limit or restrict the general subject area to a topic that can be discussed in specific terms as the theme develops. For example, the general topic "Drugs" covers too much material for a single writing. The general topic, however, offers many possible limited topics which could be developed in a theme: why start on drugs, types of drugs or one type, drugs in ancient Egypt, how far is hooked, an ex-drug addict speaks out, my personal opinion on drugs, what is a trip really like, the after effects of drugs.

If sports interests you, you might first limit the general topic "Sports" to "Basketball" and then begin to consider possible limited topics such as: the price one pays to become a good player, fundamentals of the game or a fundamental, how to shoot effectively, different kinds of shots, basketball as a profession, preparation for a game, the necessity of physical fitness, positions of the players, height as a factor in games.

The general topic "Hobbies" might be limited to "Coin Collecting," which offers the following limited topics: buying and selling coins, placing value on coins, proper care and storage of coins, profits in coin collecting, how to get started in coin collecting.

Stating the Central Idea

The central idea for a theme is similar to the topic sentence for a paragraph; both specifically identify what is to be discussed in sentences following.

Before writing, you should state exactly the central idea you will discuss. This may be done in at least two ways. First, if the writing deals with facts, you can begin with "My purpose is _____," "I intend to _____," "I will explain _____," or "The purpose of this paper is _____." Exposition (explanatory writing) and sometimes description or narration can best be *planned* by writing such a statement of purpose or intent.

> *Examples:*   I will explain how to make a kite from materials found in almost any household.

> The purpose of this paper is to explain how to make a bookcase.

> Purpose: to explain how to buy groceries on a limited budget.

Second, if the writing is about feelings, beliefs, or attitudes, you should also make a specific statement of the central idea. This statement is often called a thesis sentence.

> *Examples:*   Everyone should have a hobby.

> The methods used by some politicians to get votes are undesirable.

> Eighteen years, not twenty-one, should be recognized legally as the beginning of adulthood.

Often the thesis indicates exactly the aspects of the topic to be developed.

> *Examples:*   Living in a city has four main advantages over living in a smaller town.

> There are three basic emotional reasons for gossip: boredom, repressed anger, and jealousy.

> President Johnson did not seek reelection because of his health, the war in the Far East, and unfavorable public opinion.

The first sample above restricts the discussion to *four* main advantages of living in a city rather than a small town. The second and third sample theses go a step further; they list the major points to be discussed. The second sample limits the discussion of the basic emotional reasons for gossip to boredom, repressed anger, and jealousy. Each of these might be discussed in a separate paragraph, following introductory comments, or each might be discussed in several paragraphs. The third sample lists the possible reasons why President Johnson did not seek reelection, and each reason would be developed in the theme.

Notice that the statement of central idea has several distinct characteristics. It needs explanation; someone reading, "Everyone should have a hobby" will ask, "*Why* should everyone have a hobby?" This is the question the theme must answer. Having read the thesis, "The methods used by some politicians to get votes are undesirable," one asks, "What are these methods?" and "Why are they undesirable?" A theme developing the thesis must answer these questions. Any satisfactory sentence stating a central idea suggests specific questions that require specific answers.

The statement also has key words and phrases that remind you what must be discussed in the development of the idea. In a short thesis such as, "Everyone should have a hobby," every word is a key word; that is, it takes the whole thesis to understand the central idea. In the thesis, "The methods used by some politicians to get votes are undesirable," the key words and phrases are "methods," "politicians," "to get votes," and "undesirable."

Listing and Organizing Supporting Details

The central idea needs details to support, explain, or develop it. You should list these just as you listed possible details to support the topic sentence for the paragraph. As you think of possible ideas, jot them down. At this point, simply concentrate on listing details; organizing them will come later.

Central Idea: To perform experiments safely in chemistry lab, a student must follow prescribed safety rules.

Details to be considered in development of central idea:
   Personal conduct
   Wear dark glasses for certain operations
   Proper ventilation
   Walking, not running, in the lab
   Consideration of other students
   Proper illumination
   Proper clothing

Using sharp-edged tools
Care of equipment
Careful use of explosive or poisonous materials
Care in using equipment
Danger of loose-fitting clothing
Orderliness of laboratory
Protection of eyes
Rubber gloves for handling certain materials

Next, look over the list of details to see if there are any related points that could be grouped under general headings. From our sample list, there seem to be at least three possible headings: personal conduct, proper clothing, and safety practices while performing experiments. Several details will logically "fit" under each heading; the remaining details should be eliminated.

Personal conduct
  Walking, not running, in the laboratory
  Consideration of other students

Proper clothing
  Danger of loose-fitting clothes
  Rubber gloves for handling certain materials
  Wear tinted glasses for certain operations

Experiment-in-progress safety practices
  Proper illumination
  Proper ventilation
  Careful use of explosive or poisonous materials
  Orderliness of equipment and materials used

After studying the arrangement of details and deciding it is logical, you should revise the wording of some points so that all are stated in the same grammatical form. Stating all details in the same grammatical form helps you to use the same approach in discussing each detail, thus making the development of the main idea clear and logical.

Since the main idea states, ". . . a student *must follow* prescribed safety rules," write the details in the same imperative form.

Central idea: To perform experiments safely in chemistry lab, a student must follow prescribed safety rules.

Personal conduct
   Walk, do not run, in the laboratory.
   Be considerate of other students.

Proper clothing
   Do not wear loose-fitting clothing.
   Wear rubber gloves for handling certain materials.
   Wear tinted glasses for certain operations.
   Wear a rubber apron when handling certain acids.

Experiment-in-progress safety practices
   Be sure work is properly illuminated.
   Be sure work area is properly ventilated.
   Exercise caution in using explosive or poisonous materials.
   Arrange equipment and materials to be used in the experiment.

A final check of the arrangement of details reveals that each detail makes a definite contribution to the development of the main idea. Each grouping relates specifically to the restricted topic.

Sometimes this grouping of ideas will not be necessary. You may simply select from your list those points necessary to develop the main idea and write them as sentences.

Central Idea: I spent last summer listening to the sounds of the country.

Details to be considered:
   Animals awakening in the early morning
   Tractors plowing fields
   The rippling of the brook behind the house
   Evening silence
   Carefree children playing
   Cattle lowing in the pastures
   Crickets chirping in the late evening

From this list you might write the following sentences.

   Every morning I awoke to the sounds of the crowing roosters, barking dogs, and neighing horses.
   While lounging on the front porch, I could hear the roaring tractors plowing the fields.

The sound of children laughing as they played their country games rang sweetly in my ears.

As night fell, I went to sleep to the rhythm of the crickets chirping.

DEVELOPING THE THEME

Next, you should decide what method of development would most clearly present the selected details. There are several common methods of development to choose from, such as example or illustration, comparison and contrast, cause and effect, and definition.

Example or Illustration

Writing that uses example or illustration as a method of development generally begins with introductory material, which states the central idea, and continues with a single lengthy example or several brief examples to support the central idea. The writing might follow this outline.

Paragraph 1   Introductory material
Paragraph 2   Example 1
Paragraph 3   Example 2
Paragraph 4   Example 3

Any single example might be expanded into several paragraphs if the material to be used is quite long or if it could be presented more clearly in several paragraphs.

Progression of movement in this type of development can be marked by such transitional words and phrases as "One example," "Another example," "Once," "On another occasion," etc.

The following student themes each use example as a method to develop the central idea.

My Experience with Firearms*

First sentence is thesis sentence that limits subject and restricts writing to relating experiences with firearms. which

My experience with firearms has taught me to use extreme caution while handling them. One reason I use a great deal of caution handling firearms is that so

*Used by permission of Larry Hooper.

taught the writer "to use extreme
caution while handling them."
Sentences 2–4 identify and explain one reason to be careful.
Sentence 5 introduces example.
Sentences 6–7 relate example.
Sentences 8–10 identify and explain a reason to be careful;
sentence 10 relates example.

Sentences 1–3 identify and explain another reason for being
careful with firearms. Sentence
4 introduces example; sentences
5–6 relate example.

Sentences 1–2 identify and explain a third reason. Sentences
3–4 relate example. Sentence 5,
the concluding sentence, is a
plea for all to use caution in
handling firearms.

many people are killed every year with
what they think are unloaded guns. These
people rely only on their memory when
cleaning a gun as to whether or not the
gun is unloaded. This is very dangerous
and stupid when it takes only a second
to check and be sure. A good example of
such carelessness is an accident that happened to a friend. He was cleaning his
shotgun, which he *thought* was unloaded,
and ran the cleaning rod down the barrel
where it hit a shell, causing it to detonate.
His face was unrecognizable when he was
found. Also some foolish people have a
habit of pointing "unloaded" guns at
others. There is no way to know how
many deaths have been caused this way.
Fortunately, I was missed, but by mere
inches, by one of these people.

Another aspect of handling firearms
that has taught me caution is watching
the way some people hunt. These people
might be extremely careful cleaning their
guns, but let them step into the woods
and their personality reverses. They think
they are the only ones in the area and
shoot at whatever moves. A perfect example of this is an accident that happened during deer season. A boy and his
father were hunting and they separated
to go to their stands. Shortly afterwards
the boy saw something moving through
the woods; he shot and killed his father.

Finally, I use caution handling firearms because of the danger involved in
transporting them. Whether transporting
the gun to a car or in a car, a person
should be sure the gun is unloaded. There
is a Pontiac GTO in north Georgia with
a hole in the right floorboard. It's there
because I laid a loaded pistol on the floor
while driving down a bumpy gravel road.

If you intend to handle a firearm in any manner, use caution so that it won't be the last one you ever hold.

My Disposition*

Paragraph 1 introduces central idea.

I'm never satisfied with things as they are; I always try to improve them. I could, I suppose, give many examples to show this, but I believe the following three examples, spanning a period of some six years, will suffice to demonstrate this aspect of my disposition.

Paragraph 2 relates first example.

About six years ago, while I was in the Air Force, I had a job scheduling maintenance on aircraft, and I was constantly trying to improve the quality and quantity of the work performed. This job required that I inform the different shops of the work needed to be done by their people on each aircraft that landed and schedule people to work on these aircraft. The job required no more than that, but I felt a personal responsibility to see that my scheduling brought efficient results. In many instances, these people would want to do some other work that they felt was more important, but I made a point of knowing the priority of everything that needed to be done, and, if there was a deviation from my schedule, then I also made a point of rectifying this situation. True, I made a few enemies by doing this, but I gained a sense of satisfaction with, in my opinion, a job well done.

Paragraph 3 relates second example.

Some time later, when I first went to work for the Burroughs Corporation, I was assigned to the shipping and parts department until I could be scheduled for my original field, engineering training,

*Used by permission of Jim Chapman.

and, while maintaining this department, I instigated new methods of ordering, cataloging, and distributing parts because I was not satisfied with existing methods. The parts bins were situated in the service department, and anyone who needed some part had merely to obtain a part number and take that particular part from whatever bin it was in. Frequently, however, these bins would be empty because no one had reordered these parts. The solution was very simple; a record had to be kept of each part taken from the bins. I requested that policy be changed to require everyone taking a part from the bins to write the part number and quantity taken on a pad, and at the end of each day I analyzed the list and reordered whatever was necessary. Also, to improve the efficiency of the parts department, I recataloged many parts and sent out distributions daily rather than weekly, as was the custom.

Paragraph 4 relates third example.

Recently I bought a house and relandscaped the yard because I was not satisfied with the landscaping job that had been done. The Federal Housing Administration had contracted to have the house renovated, and the contractor had also done some work in the yard. Deep drainage ditches had been placed around the house at every conceivable angle, and not only was it almost impossible to mow the lawn but very difficult to walk outside at night without sustaining serious injury. Well, I made short work of filling in all the ditches and putting in my own drainage system, then proceeded to tear down the old fence and put up a new one, haul in a truckload of topsoil and smooth out and reseed the lawn, and cut down all the trees that didn't suit me.

I'm still not satisfied with the lawn, but I'm too tired to do anything more to it for a while. Or perhaps there comes a time when one has to be satisfied with things as they are?

Comparison and Contrast

Writing that uses comparison or contrast as a method of development usually begins with a sentence identifying the two things to be compared or contrasted and continues with a discussion of their similarities or differences. For example, in a theme showing how the games of tennis and badminton are alike, you would compare the two, emphasizing the similarities between them. In a theme showing how croquet and golf are different, you would contrast the two, emphasizing the differences, or you might use both comparison and contrast.

There are two possible arrangements of material that compares or contrasts. It may be arranged point by point; that is, you would complete each point of discussion about both items before moving to the next. For example, in a theme comparing tennis and badminton, you might arrange the material as follows:

Paragraph 1   Introductory material

Paragraph 2   First similarity: equipment needed for playing tennis and equipment needed for playing badminton

Paragraph 3   Second similarity: procedure for playing tennis and procedure for playing badminton

Paragraph 4   Third similarity: keeping score in tennis and keeping score in badminton

Or, you might use a section by section arrangement; that is, the theme would be divided into two large sections, each containing one or more paragraphs. The first section would discuss all the similarities or differences of one of the two objects, terms, or ideas identified in the central idea; the second section would discuss all the similarities or differences of the other object, term, or idea, following the points of comparison or contrast in the first section. You could arrange the same material comparing tennis and badminton as follows:

Paragraph 1	Introductory material
Paragraph 2 (or more)	Discuss all points about tennis that will be compared to badminton: equipment, procedure for playing, keeping score
Paragraph 3 (or more)	Discuss same points about badminton: equipment, procedure for playing, keeping score

There is, of course, no rule about the number of paragraphs necessary for the development or discussion of each similarity or difference. You must decide this as you consider how much material you have and how you can best present this material clearly and concisely.

The essays below use comparison and contrast as a method of development.

Of Books and Men*

Sentences 1–2 identify the objects to be compared: books and men. The remaining sentences contrast the two objects.

If I had been asked in my early youth whether I preferred to have dealings only with men or only with books, my answer would certainly have been in favor of books. In later years this has become less and less the case. Not that I have had so much better experiences with men than with books; on the contrary, purely delightful books even now come my way more often than purely delightful men. But the many bad experiences with men have nourished the meadow of my life as the noblest book could not do, and the good experiences have made the earth into a garden for me. On the other hand, no book does more than remove me into a paradise of great spirits, where my innermost heart never forgets I cannot dwell long, nor even wish that I could do so. For (I must say this straight out in

*"Books and Men" from *Pointing the Way: Collected Essays* by Martin Buber. Edited and translated from the German by Maurice Freedman. Copyright © 1957 by Martin Buber. Reprinted by permission of Harper & Row, Publishers, Inc.

order to be understood) my innermost heart loves the world more than it loves the spirit. I have not, indeed, cleaved to life in the world as I might have; in my relations with it I fail it again and again; again and again I remain guilty towards it for falling short of what it expects of me, and this is partly, to be sure, because I am so indebted to the spirit. I am indebted to the spirit as I am to myself, but I do not, strictly speaking, love it, even as I do not, strictly speaking, love myself. I do not in reality love him who has seized me with his heavenly clutch and holds me fast; rather I love her, the "world," who comes again and again to meet me and extends to me a pair of fingers.

Paragraph 2 compares the "gifts" offered by books and by men to man.

Both have gifts to share. The former showers on me his manna of books; the latter extends to me the brown bread on whose crust I break my teeth, a bread of which I can never have enough: men. Aye, these tousle-heads and good-for-nothings, how I love them! I revere books —those that I really read—too much to be able to love them. But in the most venerable of living men I always find more to love than to revere: I find in him something of this world, that is simply there as the spirit never can be there. The spirit hovers above me powerfully and pours out his exalted gift of speech, book; how glorious, how weird! But she, the human world, needs only to cast a wordless smile, and I cannot live without her. She is mute; all the prattle of men yields no word such as sounds forth constantly out of books. And I listen to it all in order to receive the silence that penetrates to me through it, the silence of the creature. But just the human creature! That creature means a mixture. Books are pure, men are mixed: books are spirit and word, pure spirit and purified word; men are made up of prattle and silence, and their silence is not that of animals but of men. Out of the human silence behind the prattle the spirit whispers to you, the spirit *as soul*. She, she is the beloved.

Paragraph 3 suggests a test to prove the author's conclusion that men are to be preferred over books.

Here is an infallible test. Imagine yourself in a situation where you are alone, wholly alone on earth, and you are offered one of the two, books or men. I often hear men prizing their solitude, but that is only because there are still men somewhere on earth, even though in the far distance. I knew nothing of books when I came forth from the womb of my mother, and I shall die without books, with another human hand in my own. I do, indeed, close my door at times and surrender myself to a book, but only because I can open the door again and see a human being looking at me.

From The Forest and the Sea*

Sentence 1 states the comparison to be made: "rain forest" to "jungle." Paragraphs 1–2 describe the "jungle" as "a green hell."

"Rain forest" and "jungle" are frequently taken to mean the same thing. But I have never liked the word jungle. It has all the wrong connotations. You hack your way painfully through the lush vegetation of the jungle, dripping sweat in the steam-bath atmosphere; snakes hang from trees and lurk under foot; leopards crouch on almost every branch and there is always a tiger just beyond the impenetrable screen of foliage. There are hordes of biting, stinging, burning things. The jungle is green hell.

*Marston Bates, from "The Rain Forest," from *The Forest and the Sea* (New York: Random House, Inc., 1960).

Sentence 1 is transitional, indicating a contrast between the "jungle" described above and the "rain forest" to be described in the following sentences.

I doubt that there is any place, outside of books and movies, where all these conditions are combined, though certainly there is plenty of nasty and difficult country, both in the tropics and out. The thickest tangle of vegetation is the second growth that springs up after the rain forest has been cleared. Everywhere in the tropics, people follow a slash-and-burn type of agriculture. Trees are felled, allowed to dry, burned, and crops planted among the charred logs. Sometimes crops are harvested for two or three years or more, but presently the land is abandoned and a new area cut. The abandoned clearing is taken over by a thick tangle of vegetation that for several years may be almost impossible to penetrate except by slow and painful cutting with a bush knife. Small mammals and rodents multiply in this vegetation, providing abundant food for the snakes that move in. Such places sometimes harbor swarms of mites, ticks, flies, mosquitoes and a wide variety of stinging things. It's about as close to a green hell as you can get.

The true rain forest, untouched, almost untrodden by man, is a different sort of place. The forest floor is open, carpeted with the richly variegated browns of many different kinds of fallen leaves, sometimes brightly spotted with blue or red or yellow from flowers that have fallen from unseen heights above. The carpeting is thin, easily scuffed away to show the red lateritic clay soil so characteristic of the equatorial regions. There is no thick accumulation of leaf mold like that of northern forests, no rich accumulation of humus. The processes of decay are too fast to permit much organic accumulation in the soil.

There is little vegetation on the forest floor since the light is too dim for plants. There is a thin growth of tree seedlings (which have no chance to grow unless some catastrophe to a forest giant should open space), ferns, sometimes dwarf palms, or scattered thickets of huge-leaved aroids, the sort of plants that also grow well in the dim light of hotel lobbies. But basically, the forest floor is open, with vistas of a hundred feet or more, vistas framed and closed by the straight trunks of the trees that disappear into the vaulted green canopy that they support above.

Paragraph compares the forest to a cathedral.

The cliche often used for the forest is "cathedral-like." The comparison is inevitable: the cool, dim light, the utter stillness, the massive grandeur of the trunks of forest giants, often supported by great buttresses and interspersed with the straight, clean columns of palms and smaller trees; the gothic detail of the thick, richly carved, woodly lianas plastered against the trunks or looping down from the canopy above. Awe and wonder come easily in the forest, sometimes exultation—sometimes, for a man alone there, fear. Man is out of scale: the forest is too vast, too impersonal, too variegated, too deeply shadowed. Here man needs his fellow man for reassurance. Alone, he has lost all significance.

Paragraph suggests a comparison between the silence of the sea and the silence of the forest. Uses personal recollection in last two sentences.

The rain forest is perhaps more truly a silent world than the sea. The wind scarcely penetrates; it is not only silent, it is still. All sound then gains a curiously enhanced mystery. A sudden crack—what could have made it? An inexplicable gurgle. A single clear peal—that was a bird, probably a trogon. A whistle, impossible to identify. But mostly silence. The silence sometimes becomes infectious; I remember sometimes trying to blend into this world by moving along a trail without rustling a leaf with my feet or popping a twig. But more often I purposely scuffled, broke noisily through this forest where I didn't belong, tried to advertise my presence both to reassure myself and to warn the creatures of the forest that a stranger was there—I had no desire to surprise a fer-de-lance.

Paragraph contrasts the reef and the forest. Uses personal recollection in sentences 3–5.

In contrast with the reef, it is a monotonously-colored world. Everything is some shade of brown or gray or green. I have lugged cameras loaded with color film all day without finding anything that seemed to warrant color photography, and in desperation, got my companions to wear red kerchiefs and blue jeans so that they could provide color contrast as well as "human interest." But I always found color photography difficult in the forest where the dim light requires long exposures, and the light itself is greatly altered by being filtered through the thick, green canopy. Only by taking advantage of the margins of clearings, or by using a flash, can you be sure of results.

Paragraph reemphasizes the "green hell" and the "cathedral" analogy.

Perhaps I am making the forest sound too easy, too open, too cathedral-like, overdoing my rebellion against the idea of jungle. It is difficult to give an objective description, to convey an accurate impression of a landscape like the rain forest which may, in one person, arouse awe and wonder, and in another, fear and hatred. P. W. Richards, in his book, *The Tropical Rain Forest,* has justly remarked that "tropical vegetation has a fatal tendency to produce rhetorical exuberance in those who describe it." The exuberance mostly tends toward the green hell side, but perhaps I have overdone the cathedral analogy.

Reemphasizes the "green hell" analogy.

I doubt whether the rain forest is anywhere easy to penetrate for any great distance. There are always obstructions: occasional fallen trunks, sudden tangled thickets, and above all, stretches of swamps and countless streams. Sometimes the streams are small, clear, shallow sandy brooks, looking no different from the forest brooks of New England, and easily negotiated. But sometimes they are broad rivers, sometimes they move sluggishly over bottomless mud, sometimes they are choked with impenetrable masses of fantastic vegetation. The green hell analogy becomes vivid enough in these forest swamps. They are the reason that man has had so little success in making trails or roads through the forests; why he clings to the major rivers either for exploration or trade.

Cause and Effect

A third possible method of development is cause and effect. Writing using this method attempts to show the relation between cause and effect. It begins with an introduction identifying the central idea. Following this, you may present the causes of the central idea and then give the results, or you may give the results first and then discuss the causes.

The following sample writing uses cause and effect as a method of development.

If a Computer Fouls Up Your Charge Account*

Paragraphs 1–4 are introductory. They identify the cause: computer billing of charge accounts. Paragraph 4 lists three questions answered in the re-

When the Lord & Taylor specialty-store chain changed its billing system a few years ago, it sent notices to charge-account customers saying, "Rejoice! Our electronic-age bill is taking over."

*Reprinted by permission from *Changing Times,* the Kiplinger Magazine, Jan., 1971. Copyright 1971 by the Kiplinger Editors, Inc., 1729 H Street, N.W., Washington, D.C. 20006. As condensed in the January 1971 *Reader's Digest.* Copyright 1970 by The Reader's Digest Assn., Inc.

maining paragraphs of the article which discuss the undesirable effects of computer billing and ways to cope with these effects.

One can be excused for doubting whether many of the store's clients actually cheered the announcement. Among the nonrejoicers, certainly, was a Washington, D.C., couple who shortly received an electronic-age bill for purchases made by a woman in West Hartford, Conn.

It's estimated that more than half of all purchases nowadays are made through charge accounts. Users of these accounts have long suffered small-to-major mixups in their bills under all kinds of billing systems. And, judging by the volume of complaints, computers and other modern marvels have made no great dent in the problem. Tell a gathering about your latest quarrel with a store, and someone there will surely be able to produce a horror story to top yours.

Why do so many errors occur? Is there some way to keep computers from mangling your account? What can you do to extricate yourself from these bill imbroglios?

Paragraphs 5–6 answer "Why do so many errors occur?"

As alive and mischievous as computers are sometimes portrayed to be, they are essentially sophisticated adding machines that must be told what to do. It is humans who prepare erroneous data for the machine, feed it the wrong reel of tape, give it wrong instructions and otherwise mislead it. The computer does, however, print out results at such headlong speed that thousands of accounts may be botched up before an error is caught. A kink in procedures is all the more serious with such big firms as oil companies, where a mistake in only a tiny fraction of their millions of credit-card accounts can cause exasperation among thousands of customers.

Paragraphs 7–12 give examples
of problems.

A slipup can leave your account in a mess at almost any point during the course of a transaction. Here are some examples of what can happen:

—The clerk checks with the credit office for an account number because the customer doesn't have her charge card. The girl in the credit office neglects to use a ruler to read across the columns from names to numbers and gives the clerk the wrong number. Some other customer gets billed.

—The salesman inserts a "$" before the total on the bill. A billing clerk reads the dollar sign as a "1" and bills $141.20 rather than $41.20.

—The customer buys $80 worth of merchandise, pays $20 in cash and charges the remainder. The clerk enters $80 in the section of the bill set aside for the total and indicates elsewhere that only $60 is to be charged. But the keypunch operator transfers only the figure in the total box to the punch cards used for posting debits and credits. The customer is billed for $80 rather than $60.

—The alteration department of a men's store doesn't coordinate its deliveries with the billing department. A customer is billed for a suit before it's even ready to wear.

—Most irritating of all, perhaps, are new mistakes made in the process of correcting old ones. A customer notifies the credit department of a discrepancy in her account. The employee who takes the call is supposed to "flag" the account to stop billing until the account is put in order. For some reason, the account isn't flagged, and the customer is billed again. Again the customer declines to pay. Now,

Paragraphs 13–14 answer "Is there some way to keep computers from mangling your account?"

according to the store's confused records, she owes a service charge. The computer dutifully calculates it and puts the customer on a delinquent-payment list.

Unfortunately, any charge account is going to get out of whack once in a while. But there are ways you can help reduce the number of errors and stop them from snowballing into a nasty mess.

1. Use your credit-card plate whenever possible, thus assuring the correct account number on the sales slip.
2. See that the figures on sales slips are correct and clear.
3. Keep duplicate sales invoices until you can compare them with your monthly statement. This is especially important when dealing with stores that use the "descriptive" billing system of summarizing transactions on the statement instead of returning the sales slips.
4. Always return the bill form or punch card with the imprinted or punched account number when you make payments, to assure proper crediting.
5. Notify a bill-sender of any error as soon as possible. Look over your monthly statements when they arrive rather than waiting until the day you pay your bills.
6. If you phone in a complaint, make a record of the name of the employee to whom you speak. That way the store can trace your case if the situation isn't cleared up.
7. If you write, don't enclose the letter with a bill payment or other correspondence; that just increases the

chances of its being lost or over-looked. Instead, send a letter by itself, preferably to a specific person in the bill-adjustment department. Include your account number and sufficient other details for the store to locate your record.

8. Don't pay any bill or part of a bill you think is wrong, and don't pay for merchandise you haven't received. When sending partial payment, write a short explanatory note, such as "Your total incorrect. Letter sent to Miss, . . ." Remember to put your name and account number on the note in case it's separated from the payment.

Allow ample time for the correction to be made, as it often takes one or two billing cycles before bill-adjusters catch up with the complaint and straighten out the records. But the error *can* be relentlessly carried forward month after month, until finally you begin receiving "collection letters," warning that your credit will be endangered or that you will become subject to legal action unless you settle the debt immediately.

Paragraphs 15–17 answer "What can you do to extricate yourself from these bill imbroglios?"

Your instinct will tell you to spring to the nearest telephone to bawl out the store. Rather than waste time calling, write to the president of the company, explaining the problem and naming the person with whom you originally communicated. (Despite some credit men's protestations that going to the top man doesn't assure you of any preferential attention, it's difficult to escape the impression that it *does* make a difference.) Send a copy of your letter to the collection agency, if one is involved, and another to the local credit bureau, asking that it be put in the credit file the bureau has on you.

You have a legal right not to be plagued for bills you don't owe, whether it's a machine or a human who labels you a deadbeat. If necessary, you can take legal action against the biller or the collection agency, or both. But you would probably have to prove that the offending organization was formally notified of its error. So send your letter by certified mail and ask for a delivery receipt.

Of course, legal action represents a last resort. If you've taken the proper precautions, and if the biller has at least a reasonable facsimile of an efficient credit department, your problem should be solved long before that time comes.

Definition

Definition is also a possible method of development. In using definition, you evaluate or identify the meaning of a word or phrase. You seek to answer the questions: What do I mean by this term? In what sense am I using this term?

Definitions may be personal, informal or formal: What is Christmas to a child? What is a hero to a soldier? What is truth? What is success? Or definitions may be scientific or technical: What is a computer? What is a laser? What is metabolism?

A definition may be a single sentence or several paragraphs. If a sentence only, the sentence should include the term defined, its class, and its distinguishing characteristic. The expanded definition may include many characteristics such as an analysis of parts, physical description, functional description, origin, history of the term, examples and illustrations, or comparison and contrast. The expanded definition states what something is by giving a full, detailed explanation of it.

The following student-written essay defines "hydroponics."

Hydroponics

Hydroponics is the science of growing plant life without soil. The mineral nutrients needed to grow plants are added to water in which the plants' roots hang freely. Several names are applied to this method of gardening: soilless agriculture, nutriculture, water culture, chemical gardening, and tank culture.

In order to grow plants by the hydroponic system, minerals must be added to the water solution about every two weeks. These mineral nutrients are calcium, phosphorous, potassium, magnesium, sulfur, and nitrogen. Small amounts of boron, zinc, copper, and manganese are also needed to keep the plants healthy.

Plants that are grown by the soilless method seem to be much healthier and produce better quality crops than plants grown in the conventional way. Many parasites, fungi, and insects attack plants grow in soil. Plants grown by hydroponics are not bothered by these pests.

A very popular form of hydroponics is growing plants in a pan or tank with oxygen circulating continuously through the water solution.

Hydrosphere is another form of hydroponics. Vegetation grows in the salt water of the ocean, about two miles down. The same chemicals are found in the salt water that must be added to the water solution for tank culture. Plants also grow in lakes and streams by the same process.

Hydroponics has been known for over one hundred years. But it was not used successfully in growing vegetation until 1938 when experiments in hydroponics were carried out on Wake Island. From these experiments soilless gardening was proved beneficial in raising green vegetables for food.

After selecting and limiting the subject, stating the central idea, listing and organizing supporting details, and choosing a method of development, the theme plan is complete, and it provides a guide to follow in writing.

WRITING THE THEME

Writing the theme involves the following: outlining, writing the rough draft, revising the rough draft, and copying the last draft.

Outlining

Listing and organizing details is a type of informal outlining that is satisfactory for any shorter theme. For most of the writing you do, this informal outlining is sufficient. A longer theme, however, will probably require a formal outline, a more detailed plan for writing. The following guides will help in writing a formal outline.

1. An outline contains a statement of the central idea and the body of the outline, which subdivides the central idea.

2. A formal outline may be topical (with single words or phrases as headlines) or sentence (with complete sentences as headlines). It should never be a combination of topic and sentence; use one *or* the other.

3. Identify main topics by Roman numerals (I, II, III, etc.); subtopics under each main topic by capital letters (A, B, C, etc.); subtopics under capital letters by Arabic numerals (1, 2, 3, etc.), and subtopics under Arabic numerals by lower case letters (a, b, c, etc.). Each group of subtopics begins farther to the right. The left margin of each group of topics begins at the same point.

I. Main topic

    A. Subtopic of I

        1. Subtopic of A
        2. Subtopic of A
        3. Subtopic of A
            a. Subtopic of 3
            b. Subtopic of 3

    B. Subtopic of I

        1. Subtopic of B
        2. Subtopic of B

    C. Subtopic of I

        1. Subtopic of C
            a. Subtopic of 1
            b. Subtopic of 1
        2. Subtopic of C

II. Main topic

    A. Subtopic of II

    B. Subtopic of II

4. Capitalize the first word of each entry.

5. Place periods after each topic number or letter. If writing a sentence outline, place a period at the end of each sentence. You may use or omit periods after entries in a topical outline.

6. Subtopics are subdivisions; therefore, you must have at least two subtopics within each group. If you have an A, you must have a B; if a 1, a 2; if an a, a b. In the one exception, listing items as illustration or example, it is possible that you might list a single item.

7. In a topical outline, state all entries of the same rank in similar form. If A is a noun clause, B and all topical entries following within that rank must be stated as noun clauses. If 1 is an infinitive phrase, 2 and all topical entries following within that rank must be infinitive phrases. In a sentence outline every entry should be a sentence.

8. Avoid a large number of main entries. Ask yourself if each entry represents a major point necessary to the development of the central idea. Cross out any unnecessary entries.

9. Be sure that each entry says something, contains information. Generally avoid such terms as *purpose, importance, benefits,* and *results.* For example, in an outline on the proper care of wash-and-wear clothing, an entry should be more specific than "One way to take proper care of wash-and-wear clothing," which gives little information. A clearer outline for this subject might look like this:

I. Machine washing provides excellent care for wash-and-wear clothing.

    A. Use cold water and the delicate cycle.

    B. Remove clothes *immediately* when cycle is completed.

    C. Hang clothes carefully, shaping them on the hanger.

Never hesitate to revise an outline. As you develop your ideas, you may discover a better arrangement; if so, change the outline. Caution: be sure the outline accompanying a final copy is actually the outline developed in the theme.

Writing the Rough Draft

Following the outline, whether formal or informal, write your first draft. This includes a beginning paragraph introducing the central idea, the body of the theme containing the supporting or developmental paragraphs for the central idea, and perhaps a closing paragraph.

Revising the Rough Draft

Any rough draft needs careful revision and correction. Often, after reading a complete theme, you may see that changes in the structure of the theme may improve its overall effectiveness. Rearranging paragraphs or sentences within paragraphs; eliminating words or groups of words which, on rereading, do not add to the development of the central idea; adding examples, facts, comparisons, or any other material that will make the meaning clearer; combining ideas originally presented in several sentences into a single sentence—such changes as these can be made during revision. You also correct errors in spelling, grammar, and punctuation.

As you look over the rough draft, ask yourself the following questions.

Words

1. Are words well chosen to convey the meaning intended?

2. Are there unnecessary words and phrases that add nothing and should be eliminated or replaced by fewer, more exact words?

3. Is each word spelled correctly?

Grammar and Punctuation

1. Is each sentence grammatically correct?

2. Does each sentence add something to the development of the supporting detail or point?

3. Is there smooth transition from sentence to sentence?

4. Are the sentences varied in length and structure?

5. Have I stated simply and clearly what I want to say?

6. Is each sentence correctly punctuated to help the reader understand the meaning intended?

Paragraphs

1. Does each paragraph contribute to the development of the central idea?

2. Is the supporting detail in each paragraph clearly explained and well developed?

3. Is there smooth and clear transition between paragraphs?

4. Are the paragraphs of proportionate length?

5. Is the method of development and the order used the most effective for the material?

If possible, it is good practice to put aside a theme for a day or two and then reread it. You may then find the need for revision that you did not notice earlier. Because it is natural for you to think that your work is good, you often don't see the need for revision. Another good practice, therefore, is to read a theme aloud to a friend or to ask a friend to read it aloud. Hearing someone else read the theme and getting his suggestions may reveal the need for more revision.

Copying the Last Draft

The final copy of the theme, the finished product, should be as "correct" as possible in grammar and mechanics, content, and development of ideas. Read the theme a final time before presenting it; there should be no errors in writing or typing and no last minute changes. It is permissible, however, to use a pen to correct small errors in typing.

SPECIAL CONSIDERATIONS IN THEME WRITING

In planning and writing a theme, you consider several special areas of construction. You should also consider the audience, point of view, word choice, grammatical usage, and sentence structure.

The Audience

Much writing appeals to a general audience. However, knowing the reader and knowing why he will read a specific piece of writing gives you the advantage of writing to suit his knowledge, interests, and needs. If the intended reader knows very little about a subject, you must try to present the material as simply as possible, defining any unknown terms and explaining all concepts mentioned. But if he knows the subject in detail, you can use terminologies and complex references without making explanations. If the intended reader is unknown, you must include all details needed for *clear* development.

While difficult to do, it is also good practice to put yourself in the reader's place, and attempt to evaluate objectively what you have written.

Point of View

Point of view is the attitude or position you take toward your subject. It may be personal: first person (I), second person (you), third person (he, she, one, the writer, the student); or it may be impersonal.

Personal		Writer's Position
First Person:	I determined that ...	Writer speaks
	I determined that you ...	Writer and reader
Second Person:	You determined that ...	Reader spoken to
Third Person:	One can determine that ...	Reader and writer
	Reviewers determined that ...	Particular group
	A critic determined that ...	An individual

Impersonal	
The purpose of this review ...	No writer or reader involvement

The least frequently used point of view is third person, passive voice.

> *Examples:* The light was turned off and the slide presentation begun.
>
> The equipment was set up in Laboratory A and each student was given a specific task in carrying out the series of experiments.

Try to avoid frequent use of the passive voice in writing because it lacks vividness. The impersonal objective point of view may be employed more effectively through the use of third person, active voice.

> *Examples:* The slide presentation proved successful after ø the elevation of the slide projector was adjusted.

> The series of experiments gave satisfactory results as each student carried out his specific test.

First person plural, "we," may also be used if "we" refers to a group.

> *Examples:* We rethreaded the projector three times before the demonstration could continue.

> We carried out the assigned tasks in completing the series of experiments underway in Laboratory A.

"We" should not be used to refer to an individual. It is pompous for one to say, "*We* believe this is the problem," when he actually means "*I* believe this is the problem." If only one person were involved in running a series of tests, he should say, "I ran the whole series of tests before reaching any conclusion," not, "*We* ran. . . ."

Once you establish a point of view, whether personal or impersonal, singular or plural, maintain it throughout the complete paragraph or theme. If you begin writing in the first person "I," continue using it. If you begin writing in the third person, active voice, do not shift to third person, passive voice. Select a point of view that will best convey your intended meaning, and use it consistently throughout.

Any shift in point of view confuses the reader and prevents effective, clear communication. Consider the following examples.

> *Different media* have many uses in the learning process. *They* can be *used* to enrich the learning experience. In the classroom *they can be used* to present the lesson. *You* can also use it to reinforce learning.

In this example, sentence 3 changes from the impersonal, objective point of view of sentences 1 and 2 to the personal, "you." To keep a consistent point of view, sentence 3 should be stated: "They can also be used to reinforce learning."

I shall first *discuss the advantages* of including students as members of policy-making committees and then the disadvantages of their inclusion *will be discussed.*

In this example, the second part of the sentence changes from the personal, active voice to the impersonal, passive voice. To be consistent in point of view, the sentence should be stated: "I shall first discuss the advantages of including students as members of policy-making committees and then I shall discuss the disadvantages of their inclusion." Or "I shall discuss the advantages and the disadvantages of including students as members of policy-making committees."

The other special considerations in theme writing (word choice and grammatical usage) demand lengthy explanation; they are discussed in the following chapters. Chapter two covered sentence structure.

5

Mechanics

Through the years certain conventions in the mechanics of written communication have developed. These conventions, or generally accepted practices, ease the communication process; for when these conventional usages are followed, the reader's attention can be rightly focused on the content of the writing. If, for instance, this paragraph were written with numerous abbreviations, without capitalization and without punctuation, the reader would have to spend a great deal of time in figuring out the words and the sentence units before he could begin to understand the subject material. The matter of mechanics, in short, is a matter of convention and of courtesy to the reader.

Following are accepted practices in the use of abbreviations, capitalization, numbers, and punctuation.

ABBREVIATIONS

It is permissible to abbreviate certain titles and terms:

- Titles preceding proper names:

Mr. (Mister), Messrs. (Mister, plural)
Mrs. (Mistress), Dr. (Doctor)

- Titles when the person's first name or initials and last name follow the title:

Lt. James W. Smith, *but* Lieutenant Smith
Rev. Arthur Bowman, *but* Reverend Bowman *or* Mr. Bowman

- Titles following proper names:

Jr. (Junior), Sr. (Senior)
M.D. (Doctor of Medicine), S.J. (Society of Jesus)

- Terms used many times in a piece of writing. The first time that the term appears, write it out in full, followed by the abbreviated form in parentheses:

10 kilograms per second (kgps); thereafter write only kgps

A Portrait of the Artist as a Young Man (*Portrait*); thereafter write only *Portrait*

• Certain terms used with numerals:

a.m. or A.M. (ante meridiem, before noon), p.m. or P.M. (post meridiem, afternoon)
Right: He arrives at 2:30 P.M.
              He arrives at 2:30 p.m.
Wrong: He arrives this P.M.

B.C. (before Christ), A.D. (anno Domini, in the year of the Lord)
Right: Julius Caesar was killed in 44 B.C.
Wrong: Julius Caesar was killed a few years B.C.

Note: The careful writer places B.C. after the date, A.D. before the date.

No. (Number)
Right: His box is No. 6.
Wrong: He does not have a box no.

$ (Dollars)
Right: The book cost $12.50.
Wrong: The book cost several $.

Other generally accepted practices concerning abbreviations include the following:

• Add "s" to some abbreviations to indicate more than one; others do not require the "s:"

Abbreviations adding "s":   6 pts. (pints)
                              Figs. (Figures) 1 and 2
                              10 lbs. (pounds)
                              20 vols. (volumes)

Abbreviations without "s":   100 mph (miles per hour)
20 rpm (revolutions per minute)
pp. (pages)
ff. (and following)

• Generally use lower-case letters for abbreviations except for abbreviations of proper nouns:

Ph.D. (Doctor of Philosophy)
Btu (British thermal unit)
UN (United Nations)

• Generally write abbreviations of organizations and governmental divisions without periods and with no space between the capital letters:

FBI (Federal Bureau of Investigation)
ABC (American Broadcasting Company)
ATS (American Technical Society)

• Avoid using contractions in formal writing. These shortened, or abbreviated, forms (doesn't, isn't) are associated with colloquial, or conversational, English.

Note: Always consult a recent dictionary for forms you are not sure about. Some dictionaries list abbreviations together in a special section; other dictionaries list abbreviated forms as regular entries in the body of the dictionary.

CAPITALIZATION

There are very few absolute rules concerning capitalization. Many reputable publishers and businesses, for instance, have their own established practices as to which words they capitalize. However, the following are basic conventions in capitalization which most people follow.

• Capitalize proper names:

Names of people and titles referring to specific persons:

Frank Lloyd Wright   Mr. Chairman
Aunt Marian   the Governor

Places (geographic locations, streets):

Canada	Golden Gate Bridge
the South	Canal Street
the Nile River	the Smoky Mountains

Races, organizations, institutions, and members of each:

Indian	Bear Creek High School
International Imports, Inc.	a Boy Scout
Chamber of Commerce	a Rotarian

Days of the week, months of the year, special days, and historic events:

Monday	Halloween
January	Middle Ages
New Year's Day	Revolutionary War

Religions and religious groups:

Judaism
United Methodist Church

Names of the Deity and personal pronouns referring to the Deity:

God	Son of God
Creator	His, Him, Thee, Thy, Thine

The pronoun I.

Capitalize:

• The first word and all other words within a title except articles (a, an, the), short prepositions (of, by, in, with), and conjunctions (and, or, but):

Just Between Us (title of a publication)
Duke of Windsor (title of a person)
The Sound of Music (title of a musical composition)
Madonna and Child (title of a painting)

• The first word of a sentence, a group of words understood as a sentence, a direct quotation, and a line of poetry:

Not now. Come back later.

"Happy families are all alike," said Tolstoi; "every unhappy family is unhappy in its own way."

• Words like "Figure," "Table," "Number" (whether written out or abbreviated) when they are used with a numeral:

No. 866819   Fig. 381 *or* Figure 381

• Trade names:

Teflon   Plymouth automobile

• Derivatives of proper names if the derivative is commonly associated with the original name:

English pewter   morocco leather
                            but
Shakespearean sonnet   pasteurized milk

• Vivid personifications:

Father Time   Mother Nature
Fate

Avoid unnecessary capitalization:

• Do not capitalize seasons of the year:

spring   summer

• Do not capitalize names of school subjects unless the name contains a proper noun or is followed by a numeral:

American history   French
science   Chemistry 301

• Do not capitalize directions:

Go three blocks south; then turn west.

• Do not capitalize names indicating kinship unless they are used in place of a proper name. Names of kinship preceded by an article or possessive are common nouns and are not capitalized:

Every summer my aunt and uncle visit us.

Every summer Aunt Jane and Uncle Bob visit us.

This year each mother and father will be sent a special invitation.

Because of Mom's back injury, she and Dad will not be able to attend the banquet.

NUMBERS

The problem with numbers is knowing when to use numerals and when to use words.

Use numerals (figures):

• For street addresses, telephone numbers, dates, measurements, time, mathematical expressions, and the like:

600 Race Street	8½-by-11-inch paper
July 30, 1971 *or* 30 July 1971	9:30 p.m.
$3.95	61 percent
25 cents each	Chapter 12, p. 14

• For numbers above ninety-nine or for numbers that require three or more written words:

100 *or* one hundred	6000 *or* 6,000 *or* six thousand
101	15,280

• When several numbers (including fractions) occur within a sentence or within related sentences:

The recipe calls for 3 cups of sugar, ½ teaspoon of salt, 2 sticks of butter, and ¼ cup of cocoa.

The report for this week shows that our office received 127 telephone calls, 200 letters, 30 personal visits, and 3 telegrams.

• For one of two numbers occuring next to each other:

1621 Forty-second Street	12 fifty-gallon containers

Use words:

• For a number or related numbers that begin a sentence:

Fifty cents is a fair entrance fee.

Sixty to seventy percent of our students come from this area.

Note: If using words for a number at the beginning of a sentence is awkward, recast the sentence.

Unacceptable: 1942 freshmen are enrolled this semester.

Awkward: Fourteen hundred ninety-two freshmen are enrolled this semester.

Acceptable: This semester 1492 freshmen are enrolled.

• For numbers that are approximate or indefinite:

If I had a million dollars, I'd buy a castle in Ireland.

About five hundred machines were returned because of faulty assembling.

• For numbers below one hundred or for numbers that require only one or two written words:

thirty-five   three hundred *or* 300

• For fractions:

The veneer is one-eighth inch thick.

Our club receives three-fourths of the general appropriation.

PUNCTUATION

Punctuation is a necessary part of language because readers and writers have to depend on these markers for preventing vagueness, indicating pauses and stops, separating and setting off various sentence elements, indicating questions and exclamations, and emphasizing main points while subordinating less important sentence content.

This section of the handbook provides a guide to accepted practices in the use of punctuation marks. For easy use the material is arranged alphabetically by the name of the punctuation mark: apostrophe, brackets, colon, comma, dash, ellipsis, exclamation point, hyphen, italics, parentheses, period, question mark, quotation marks, and semicolon.

Apostrophe (')

The apostrophe is used to:

- Take the place of a letter or letters in a contraction:

I'm (I am)   We've (we have)

- Show the possessive form of singular nouns and indefinite pronouns:

citizen's responsibility   someone's book

Note: To form the possessive of a singular noun add the apostrophe + s.

doctor + ' + s = doctor's, as in doctor's advice

If a singular proper noun ends in an *s* sound, add the apostrophe alone if the proper noun is multi-syllabic; add the apostrophe + s if the proper noun is one syllable.

Socrates' philosophy   Keats's poems

Note: Personal pronouns (his, hers, its, theirs, ours, yours) do not need the apostrophe because they are already possessive by form.

- Show the possessive form of plural nouns:

boys' coats   children's shoes

Note: To show plural possessive, first make the noun plural; if the plural noun ends in *s*, add only an apostrophe. If the plural noun does not end in *s*, add an apostrophe + s.

- Form the plurals of numbers, letters, and words used as words:

I cannot distinguish between your *3's* and *5's*.
Don't use too many *and's*, and eliminate *I's* from your report.

Note: The apostrophe may be omitted if there is no possibility of misreading.

Brackets ([   ])

Brackets are used rarely in writing. Their main use is in quotations, to enclose comments or explanations not written by the original author:

"Good design [of automobiles] involves efficient operation, sound construction, and pleasing form."

Colon (:)

The colon, primarily a mark of introduction, is used to:

- Introduce a list or series of items:

Many countries of the world have natural resources: iron, copper, tin, coal, rare metals and elements, rubber, and wool.

- Introduce a clause that explains, reinforces, or gives an example of a preceding clause or expression:

American industry uses the English system of linear measure as standard: the common unit of length is the inch.
"Keep cool: it will be all one a hundred years hence." (Emerson)

- Introduce a long or formal quotation:

My argument is based on George Meredith's words: "The attitudes, gestures and movements of the human body are laughable in exact proportion as that body reminds us of a mere machine."

- Introduce an emphatic word, phrase, or clause:

We have overlooked the most obvious motive: love.
That leaves me with one question: when do we start?

- Follow a formal greeting (usually in a business letter):

Dear Mr. Bozeman: Gentlemen:

- Indicate such relationships as ratio, time, and volume and page:

40:1   2:50 a.m.
x:y   42:81–90   (volume 42, pages 81–90)

Comma (,)

The comma, the most commonly used punctuation mark, generally either separates or sets off material. The comma is used to:

- Separate items in a series:

Abraham Lincoln believed in a government of the people, by the people, and for the people.

Note: The comma preceding the "and" of the last item may be omitted.

- Separate independent clauses connected with a coordinate conjunction:

There was a time when the housewife had few interests outside the home, but today she is a leader in local and national affairs.

- Separate words that may be misread:

Besides Sharon, Ann is the only available organist.

- Separate long introductory, modifying phrases and clauses from the remainder of the sentence:

In illustrating the many known uses of the laser, the scientist repeatedly emphasized its potential.
Whenever I learn to do a particular thing well, I find that I have a renewed confidence in myself.

- Separate units in a number of four or more digits (except telephone numbers, zip numbers, house numbers, and the like):

2,560,781   7,868 *or* 7868

- Separate two adjectives of equal emphasis and with the same relationship to the noun modified:

The philanthropist made a generous, unexpected gift to our college.

Note: If "and" can be substituted for the comma or if the order of the adjectives can be reversed, without violating the meaning, the adjectives are of equal rank and a comma is needed.

- Set off each item after the first in an address:

Last year Boulder, Colorado, was the convention site.

Report to me at 1045 Aspen Street, Cleveland, Ohio, for your new assignment.

• Set off the year from the day in a date:
October 26, 1963, is his birth date.

Note: If the day precedes the month, omit the commas.
On 26 October 1963 he was born.

Note: The comma between the month and the year (without the day of the month) is optional.

In July 1969 (or July, 1969,) man first landed on the moon.

• Set off any material in a sentence that is not essential to the basic sentence meaning; this nonessential material (word, phrase, or clause) may give added information, or it may be a sentence interrupter or a parenthetical expression:

James Baldwin, who was born in New York, is a prominent contemporary writer.
Yes, you may go.
African violets, on the other hand, are very delicate flowers.

• Set off appositives:

Sacramento, the capital of California, is in the northern part of the state.
We listened to the sound, eerie and mystifying.

Note: Setting off an appositive that is a proper noun is optional.

The book *Robinson Crusoe* is still a delight to readers.
The book, *Robinson Crusoe*, is still a delight to readers.

• Set off contrasting elements:

Fred, not David, is the older boy.
The harder we work, the sooner we will finish.
You will write me, won't you?

• Set off the name of the person or thing addressed:

If you can, Miss Yates, I would like for you to attend the meeting.
My dear car, we are going to have a good time this weekend.

- Set off the "he said" (or similar) matter in a direct quotation:

"I am going," Mary responded.
"If you need help," he said, "a student assistant will be in the library."

- Set off the abbreviation for *incorporated* or *limited* from a company name:

Drake Enterprises, Inc., is our major competitor.
I believe that Harrells, Ltd., will answer our request.

- Set off a title following a person's name:

Tomorrow James R. Riley, Jr., will announce the winner.
Patton A. Houlihan, President of Irish Imports, is here.

- Follow the salutation in a *social* letter and the complimentary close of *every* letter:

Dear Mother,   Yours truly,
Dear Lynne,   Sincerely,

Note: The salutation in a business letter is followed by a colon.

- Indicate understood words in an elliptical clause:

Tom was elected president; Jill, vice-president.

Dash (—)

The dash, seldom used in formal writing, generally indicates emphasis or a sudden break in thought. Often the dash is interchangeable with a less strong punctuation mark: if emphasis is desired, use a dash; if not, use the alternate punctuation mark (usually comma, colon, or parentheses).

Use dashes to:

- Set off material for emphasis:

I want one thing out of this course—a passing grade.
My father—he is first vice-president of the company—will call this to the attention of the board of directors.
I was overwhelmed—yes, completely overwhelmed—at receiving the award.

• Separate a summarizing clause from a series:

Tests, a term paper, and class participation—these are the factors that determine your grade.

Note: The summarizing clause usually begins with "these," "those," or "such."

• Set off, for clarity, long appositives and to set off parenthetical matter requiring a question mark or exclamation point:

Four major factors—cost, color, fabric, and fit—influence the purchase of a suit of clothes.
If we should succeed—God help us!—all mankind will profit.

• Mark a sudden break or shift in thought:

The murderer is—but perhaps I shouldn't spoil the book for you.
A fuller explanation is essential—but we don't have time for it today.

Ellipsis (... or ....)

Ellipsis (plural form: ellipses) periods are used to indicate that words have been left out of quoted material. Three periods are used to show that words have been omitted at the beginning of a quoted sentence and within a quoted sentence. Four periods are used to show that words have been omitted at the end of a quoted sentence, the fourth period being the period at the end of the sentence.

"The average American family spent about $2100 on food . . . in 1968."
"The adoption of standard time in North America stems from the railroads' search for a solution to their chaotic schedules. . . . In November, 1883, rail companies agreed to set up zones for each 15 degrees of longitude, with uniform time throughout each zone."

Exclamation Point (!)

The exclamation point is used to show sudden or strong emotion or force, or to mark the writer's surprise:

> What a day!
> The computer (!) made a mistake.

Hyphen (-)

The hyphen is used to separate parts of:

- Compound adjectives when they precede the word modified:

  an eighteenth-century dramatist   pro-Capitalist policy
  absent-minded professor   40-hour week

- Compound nouns:

brother-in-law	vice-president
passer-by	4-H Club
U-turn	kilowatt-hour

  Note: Many compound nouns are written as a single word, such as "notebook" and "blueprint." Others are written as two words without the hyphen, such as "card table" and "steam iron." If you do not know how to write a word, look it up in a dictionary.

- Compound verbs, usually:

  brake-test   oven-temper

- Compound numbers and fractions when they are written out:

  seventy-four people   one-eighth of an inch

- A word divided at the end of a line:

  When we arrived at the kinder-
  garten, the children were gone.

- Some words whose prefix is separated from the main stem of the word:

ex-president	self-respect
semi-invalid	half-tone

Note: A good dictionary is the best guide for determining which words are hyphenated.

Italics (underlining)

Italics (*such as these words*) are used in print; the equivalent in handwriting is underlining. Italics differentiate words and passages from the remainder of the sentence; quotation marks may also be used for the same purpose.

Italicize (underline):

● Titles of books, magazines, newspapers, long poems, plays, musical compositions, motion pictures, ships, trains, and aircraft:

> At the library yesterday I checked out the book *Madame Bovary,* read this month's *Harper's,* looked at the sports section in the *Daily Register,* and listened to *My Fair Lady.*

> The *Maid Marian* sails at dawn.

> *Note:*   Do not italicize Bible nor the names of the books of the Bible.

● Words, letters, or figures when they are referred to as such:

> People often confuse *to* and *too.*
> I cannot distinguish between your *a's* and *o's.*

● Words and phrases that are considered foreign:

> His novel is concerned with the *nouveau riche.*
> *but* This item is included gratis. (The last word in this sentence is no longer considered foreign.)

● A word or phrase for special emphasis. If the emphasis is to be effective, however, italics must be used sparingly.

> My final word is *no.*

Parentheses (   )

Always used in pairs, parentheses are used to:

- Enclose material remotely connected with the remainder of the sentence:

> If I can find a job (and I probably can), I will pay part of my school expenses.
> Ernest Hemingway (1899–1961) won the Nobel Prize in literature.

> *Note:* In some sentences the writer may have a choice between using parentheses or dashes. Dashes emphasize the words set off; parentheses subordinate them.

- Enclose letters or numbers that mark items in a list:

> Government surveys indicate that students drop out of school because they (1) dislike school, (2) think it would be more fun to work, and (3) need money for themselves and their families.

- Enclose material within a sentence directing the reader to look at other pages, charts, figures, etc:

> The average life expectancy in the United States is seventy years (see Fig. 3).

Period (.)

The period is used to:

- Mark the end of declarative and imperative sentences:

> The test is scheduled for Wednesday.
> Bring a notebook to class.

- Follow initials and some abbreviations:

> Dr. H. J. Wright, Jr.   p. 31
> Mr. John T. Parsons   4:37 p.m.

- Mark decimals:

> $10.52
> A reading of 1.260 indicates a full charge in a battery; 1.190, a half charge.

- Follow number and letter symbols in an outline:

I.
  A.
  B.
II.

Question Mark (?)

The question mark is used to:

- Follow interrogative sentences (sentences that ask questions):

Did you answer the telephone?

- Indicate there is some question as to certainty or accuracy:

Chaucer 1343(?)–1400
The spindle should revolve at a slow (?) speed.

Quotation Marks ("   ")

Quotation marks, always in pairs, are used to:

- Enclose every direct quotation:

The doctor said, "Stay in bed and rest for at least a week."
The *American Heritage Dictionary* defines a dulcimer as "a musical instrument with wire strings of graduated lengths stretched over a sound box, played with two padded hammers or by plucking."

- Enclose titles of magazine articles, book chapters, short poems, songs, and the like:

Have you read "The Population Explosion" in the current issue of *Newsweek* or "If" by Rudyard Kipling?

Note: Titles of magazines and books are underlined (italicized in print).

- Distinguish words on a different level of usage:

The ambassador and his delegation enjoyed the "good country eating."

Use quotation marks properly with other marks of punctuation:

• The closing quotation mark always follows the period or comma:

"File all applications before May," the director of personnel cautioned, "if you wish to be considered for summer work."

• The closing quotation mark always precedes the colon or semicolon:

I have just finished reading Edgar Allan Poe's story, "The Murders in the Rue Morgue"; the solution to the murders is almost unbelievable.

• The closing quotation mark precedes the question mark, exclamation point, or dash when they are a part of the quoted material. The closing quotation mark follows the question mark, exclamation point, or dash when they refer to the entire sentence:

Bill asked, "Did you receive the telegram?"
Who said, "I cannot be here tomorrow"?
Was it you who yelled, "Fire!"?

• Use single quotation marks (' ') for a quotation within a quotation:

Mother replied, "I distinctly heard your father say, 'You may use the car on weekends but not on school nights.'"
This writer states, "Of all Poe's poetry, 'The Bells' is the most musical."

• At the beginning of a theme do not put the title in quotation marks (unless the title is a quotation).

My first date.
The Enduring Popularity of "White Christmas."

Semicolon (;)

The semicolon is used to:

• Separate independent clauses *not* joined by a coordinate conjunction (and, but, or):

Germany has a number of well-known universities; several of them have been in existence since the Middle Ages.

Note: Short or emphatic clauses may be separated by commas.

I came, I saw, I conquered.

• Separate independent clauses joined by a transitional connective. Transitional connectives include such conjunctive adverbs as "also," "however," "moreover," "nevertheless," "then," "thus" and such explanatory expressions as "for example," "in fact," "on the other hand."

We have considered the historical background of the period; thus we can consider its cultural achievements more intelligently.

During the Renaissance the most famous Humanists were from Italy; for example, Petrarch, Boccaccio, Ficino, and Pico della Mirandello were all of Italian birth.

• Separate items in a series containing internal punctuation:

Our itinerary included London, Ontario, Canada; Washington, D.C., U.S.A.; and Tegucigalpa, Honduras, Central America.

• Separate two independent clauses joined by a coordinate conjunction when the clauses contain internal punctuation or when the clauses are long:

The room needs a rug, new curtains, and a lamp; but my budget permits only the purchase of a lamp.
"In theory there is nothing to hinder our following what we are taught; but in life there are many things to draw us aside." (Epictetus)

• Separate a list of examples from the preceding independent clause when the list is introduced by "that is," "for example," "for instance," or a similar expression.

Many great writers have had to overcome severe physical handicaps; for instance, John Milton, Alexander Pope, and James Joyce.

6

Vocabulary, Spelling, and Word Choice

Rightly or wrongly, people judge a person's education and intelligence on the basis of his vocabulary, spelling, and word choice. Both in school and out, using words inappropriately puts you at a disadvantage.

This chapter stresses vocabulary growth through effective use of the dictionary. Suggestions for improving spelling are presented through discussing formation of plurals, use of "ie" and "ei," spelling changes when affixes are added, and use of "ceed," "cede," "sede." The concluding section deals with word choice: denotation and connotation, specific and general words, conciseness, and words often confused and misused.

VOCABULARY

Since perhaps the best guide to an increased vocabulary is the dictionary, you should learn how to use it effectively.

Unabridged and Abridged Dictionaries

Dictionaries are classified as either unabridged or abridged. The unabridged dictionary contains extensive information about the most often used words in a language. Perhaps the most authoritative unabridged dictionaries in the English language are the multi-volume *Oxford (New) English Dictionary* (Oxford, England: Oxford University Press) and the *Dictionary of American English on Historical Principles* (Chicago: University of Chicago Press). Other unabridged dictionaries are the *New Standard Dictionary of the English Language* (New York: Funk and Wagnalls), *Random House Dictionary of the English Language* (New York: Random House), *Webster's New Twentieth Century Dictionary* (New York: World Publishing Company), and *Webster's Third New International Dictionary of the English Language* (Springfield, Mass.: G. & C. Merriam Company).

The dictionary referred to most often is the abridged or shortened dictionary, often called a desk dictionary. Among the several reliable up-to-date desk dictionaries are *The American College Dictionary* (New York: Random House), *The American Heritage Dictionary of the English Language* (Boston: Houghton Mifflin Company; New York: American Heritage Publishing Company, Inc.), *Funk and Wagnalls Standard Desk Dictionary* (New York: Funk and Wagnalls), *Standard College Dictionary* (New York: Harcourt Brace Jovanovich), *Webster's New World Dictionary of the American Language*, Modern Desk Edition (New York: World Publishing Company), and *Webster's Seventh New Collegiate Dictionary* (Springfield, Mass.: G. & C. Merriam Company).

You should avoid being misled by cheap dictionaries that contain inadequate and out-of-date information. Guides in determining the reliability of a dictionary include a recent, *complete-revision* date (not merely a recent copyright date), an adequate number of words entered, and sufficient information for each word entry. A word entry in a standard dictionary (as explained in the following pages) contains the word divided into syllables, all acceptable spellings of the word, all acceptable pronunciations with diacritical and stress marks, parts of speech, inflected forms, all commonly used definitions with subject labels for specific fields, and the origin of the word.

Information in the Dictionary

No standard order or format exists for the information within a dictionary. Therefore, you should familiarize yourself with your dictionary by referring to the introductory guide pages and table of contents.

WORD ENTRY—TYPICAL INFORMATION

A typical word entry (see illustration*) contains the following information.

[Handwritten annotations: 1. Entry word divided into syllables. / 2. Pronunciation / 3. Parts of Speech / 4. Inflected Forms / 5. Definition / 6. Etymology]

boo·mer·ang (boo′mə-răng′) *n.* 1. A flat, curved wooden missile, some types of which can be hurled so that they return to the thrower. It is used as a weapon by Australian aborigines. 2. A statement or course of action that rebounds detrimentally against its originator. —*intr.v.* **boomeranged, -anging, -angs.** To result in adverse effect upon the originator; to backfire. [Native Australian word, variously recorded as *wo-mur-rang,* hu*marin.*]

1. *Entry word divided into syllables.* In most dictionaries syllables of words are separated by centered dots. Syllable division is an important key in spelling and pronunciation. If the entry word has more than one spelling, all spellings are given. Check the guide pages in the dictionary to determine preferred spellings.

2. *Pronunciation.* Following the syllabicated entry word is the pronunciation (in parentheses) with diacritical and stress marks. Diacritical marks or symbols, explained at the bottom of the page or on the front or back endpaper of your dictionary, represent various sounds. Stress marks indicate syllables accented in pronunciation. Most dictionaries use a heavy stress mark (′) to indicate the syllable to receive the greatest emphasis in pronunciation and a lighter stress mark (′) to indicate the syllable to receive less emphasis. A word may have several pronunciations. Sometimes the pronunciation used most frequently is placed first, sometimes last. Check the guide pages in the dictionary for an explanation of pronunciation.

3. *Parts of speech.* For each word entry, the part or parts of speech are listed.

4. *Inflected forms.* Plurals of nouns, cases of pronouns, principal

*This example and all other examples from a dictionary are from *The American Heritage Dictionary of the English Language.* © Copyright 1969, 1970, 1971 by American Heritage Publishing Company, Inc.

parts of verbs, and comparisons of adjectives and adverbs are given, particularly if the forms vary greatly.

5. *Definitions.*   Many words have several definitions, some of which may be used more commonly than the others. Some dictionaries list the more common or earlier meanings first; other dictionaries list them last. Also, words may have different meanings when applied to specific fields; these special meanings are usually preceded by a subject label.

6. *Etymology.*   Etymology is the origin and historical development of a word. This information [given in brackets] may precede or follow the definition. Explanation of the abbreviations and symbols used in the etymology will be found in the guide pages in the dictionary.

WORD ENTRY—ADDITIONAL INFORMATION

Besides the syllabicated entry word, pronunciation, parts of speech, inflected forms, definitions, and etymology, additional information may be given for a particular word (see illustration for the dictionary entry *book*). These kinds of additional information include the following.

7. Abbreviations

book (book) *n. Abbr.* **b., B., bk. 1.** A volume made up of written or printed pages fastened along one side and encased between protective covers. **2.** Any written or printed literary work. **3.** A bound volume of blank or ruled pages. **4. a.** Any of the volumes in which financial transactions are recorded. **b.** *Plural.* Such records collectively. **5.** A main division of a larger written or printed work: *a book* of the Old Testament. **6.** A libretto (*see*). **7.** The script of a play. **8.** *Capital* **B.** The Bible. Often used with *The.* **9.** A set of standards, rules, conventions, or policies. Used with *the: He runs the company by the book.* **10.** *Plural. Informal.* Studies; lessons. Used with *the.* **11.** Something regarded as a source of knowledge: *the book of life.* **12.** A small packet of similar items bound together: *a book of matches.* **13.** A record of bets

9. Cross References

8. Special Meanings

10. Usage Labels

11. Subject Labels

8. Special Meanings

10. Usage Labels

12. Idiomatic Usage

9. Cross References

placed on a race. **14.** *Card Games.* The number of tricks needed before any tricks can have scoring value, as the first six tricks taken by the declaring side in bridge. **15.** A bundle of tobacco leaves sliced lengthwise. —**bring to book. 1.** To compel to explain or account for. **2.** To reprimand. —**by the book.** According to established rules. —**close the books. 1.** *Bookkeeping.* To make no further entries in and to draw up statements from the records as they stand. **2.** To bring to an end. —**in one's book.** In one's opinion. —**keep books.** To keep financial records of. —**like a book.** Thoroughly: completely: *She knows him like a book.* —**make book.** *Slang.* To accept bets as a bookmaker, especially on a sporting event. —**one for the books.** *Informal.* Something noteworthy. —**on the books. 1.** Recorded or registered. **2.** Enlisted or enrolled. —**throw the book at.** *Slang.* **1.** To make all possible charges against (an offender or lawbreaker, for example). **2.** To reprimand or punish severely. —*tr.v.* **booked, booking, books. 1.** To list or register in or as if in a book. **2.** To record charges against (a person) on a police blotter. **3.** To arrange for in advance; reserve (tickets, for example). **4.** To hire (entertainers, for example). [Middle English *bok,* Old English *boc,* written document composition. See **bhago-** in Appendix.*]

7. *Abbreviations.* Various ways of abbreviating the word may be given.

8. *Special meanings.* Often a word takes on a special meaning when capitalized or used in the plural, in a phrase, or, especially, in a particular field.

9. *Cross references.* The reader is directed to "see" or "see also" a related word entry or section in the dictionary for additional information.

10. *Usage labels.* Many dictionaries identify words and their definitions according to the level or style of language usage. Common usage labels include *archaic* (old-fashioned, outdated), *British* (used especially in Great Britain), *colloquial* (everyday, conversational), *dialect* (special to a specific locality), *informal* (belonging to the usage of natural spoken language), *nonstandard* (outside of standard, educated speech), *rare* (seldom used), *slang* (used in place of conventional terms to effect a light, humorous, or extreme tone), *vulgar* (illiterate).

> *Note:* Remember that the listing of a word in the dictionary is not an endorsement of unrestricted usage. A dictionary simply *records* the ways words are used; it does *not dictate* acceptable and unacceptable usage.

11. *Subject labels.* A subject label indicates a specialized meaning for a particular field or activity.

12. *Idiomatic usage.* An idiom is a word or phrase peculiar to a language. Such usage is natural to the native speaker of a particular language.

SPECIAL SECTIONS IN THE DICTIONARY

Other information is often included in the dictionary either as word entries or in special sections. Such additional information may be illustrations, synonyms and antonyms, biographical notations, foreign words and phrases, geographical locations, abbreviations, signs and symbols, forms of address, idiomatic phrases and expressions, and spelling rules.

Improving Your Vocabulary

You can increase your vocabulary significantly by following a few simple suggestions:

- *Write down unfamiliar words*, while listening and reading, to be looked up. Later as you look up the words in a dictionary, find the meaning most suitable for the particular usage.

- *Underline as you read*, marking words that are new to you, especially those that recur in the piece. Look up the words in a dictionary.

- *Try to figure out the meaning of a word by its context*, that is, by its use with the surrounding words. It is always a good idea, however, to check a supposed definition in a dictionary.

- *Note common prefixes, suffixes, and base words.* Many of these come from the Latin, Greek, and Germanic languages. Familiarity with a core list of prefixes, suffixes, and base words can help immeasurably in figuring out the meanings of words.

- *Ask for words to be explained.* In conversation, in class, or elsewhere when it is appropriate to do so, ask the speaker to explain the meaning of words you do not understand.

- *Make use of a good vocabulary manual.* A planned program of vocabulary development with detailed suggestions can be of great value in improving your vocabulary.

- *Use the words you learn.* Without being showy, manage to use immediately in your speaking and writing the new words that you learn, for this practice will help to establish these words in your vocabulary.

SPELLING

Because of the strong influence of other languages, spelling in the English language is fairly irregular.

If you are currently having difficulty with spelling, here are several helpful suggestions:

- *Keep a study list of words misspelled.* Review the list often, dropping words that you have learned to spell and adding any new spelling difficulties.

- *Attempt to master the spelling of these words from the study list.* Use any method that is successful for you. Some students find that writing one or several words on a card and studying them while riding to school or waiting between classes is an effective technique. Some relate the word in some way, such as "There is 'a rat' in sep*arat*e."

- *Be careful in pronouncing words.* Most persons tend to write words as they say them or hear them. For example, the writing of *prompness* instead of *promptness* probably results from a problem in pronunciation or hearing.

- *Use a dictionary.* It is the poor speller's best friend. If you have some idea of the correct spelling of a word but are not sure, consult a dictionary. If you have no idea about the correct spelling, get someone to help you find the word in a dictionary. Or look in a dictionary designed for poor spellers, which lists words by their common misspellings and then gives the correct spelling.

- *Proofread everything you write.* Look carefully at every word within a piece of writing. Even if a word just does not "look right," check its spelling in a dictionary.

SPELLING RULES

Although spelling may be difficult, it can be mastered—primarily because many spelling errors are a violation of conventional practices for forming the plurals of nouns; use of "ie" and "ei"; spelling changes when affixes are added; and use of "ceed," "cede," and "sede."

Forming the Plurals of Nouns

The most important thing to remember is this: when in doubt about the plural form of a word, consult a dictionary.

- Most nouns simply add *s* to form the plural.

    boat—boats   window—windows

- Nouns ending in *ch*, *sh*, *s*, *x*, or *z* require *es* to form the plural.

    church—churches   mash—mashes
    gas—gases   tax—taxes
                        buzz—buzzes

- Although most nouns ending in *f*, *fe*, or *ff*, add *s* to form their plural, about a dozen nouns require a change of *f* or *fe* to *ves*.

    belief—beliefs   elf—elves
    chief—chiefs   half—halves
    roof—roofs   wife—wives
    scarf—scarfs (or scarves)   wolf—wolves

- Nouns ending in *o* form their plurals in one of two ways:

1. Nouns ending in *o* preceded by a vowel and nouns denoting musical terms usually require *s* to form the plural.

  radio—radios alto—altos
  zoo—zoos   soprano—sopranos

2. Nouns ending in *o* preceded by a consonant usually require *es* to form the plural.

  hero—heroes   veto—vetoes
  potato—potatoes volcano—volcanoes

  Exceptions: photos, tobaccos, zeros

- Nouns ending in *y* form plurals in one of two ways:

1. Nouns ending in *y* preceded by a vowel usually require *s* to form the plural.

  day—days valley—valleys

2. Nouns (except proper nouns) ending in *y* preceded by a consonant require the *y* changed to *i* and the addition of *es*.

  army—armies cry—cries

- A very few nouns form the plural by adding *en* or *ren*.

  ox—oxen child—children

- Seven nouns form the plural by an internal vowel change. These umlaut plurals are the following:

  man—men   tooth—teeth
  woman—women louse—lice
  foot—feet   mouse—mice
  goose—geese

- Hyphened and phrase compounds are usually pluralized in the main word. Compounds written as one word are usually pluralized as if they were noncompounds.

  brother-in-law—brothers-in-law handful—handfuls
  passer-by—passers-by   textbook—textbooks

● A number of words borrowed from other languages retain their foreign plurals. Many of these borrowed nouns may also form the plural by adding the conventional *s* or *es*.

1. Some singular Latin nouns end in *um*; in the plural the *um* is changed to *a*.

datum—data   bacterium—bacteria
addendum—addenda   stratum—strata
medium—media or mediums   memorandum—memoranda
                                  or memorandums

2. Some singular Latin forms end in *is;* in the plural the *is* becomes *es*.

analysis—analyses   basis—bases
crisis—crises   synopsis—synopses

3. The Latin feminine form *alumna* becomes *alumnae* in the plural; the masculine form *alumnus* becomes *alumni* in the plural.

● The plurals of letters, numbers, signs, and words used as examples are formed by adding *'s* (the apostrophe may be omitted if there is no possibility of misreading).

The sentence has too many *and's* and *but's.*
I can't distinguish between your *o's* and *a's.*
All *13s* (or *13's*) have been omitted in the numbering system.

Using "ie" and "ei"

The following jingle sums up most of the guides for correct *ie* and *ei* usage:

Use *i* before *e,*
Except after *c,*
Or when sounded like *a,*
As in *neighbor* and *weigh.*

● Use *ei* when the sound is *a.*

freight   neighbor
reign   weigh
sleigh   vein

- Generally use *ei* after *c*.

    deceive   receive

An exception occurs when the combination of letters *cie* is sounded *sh*; in such instances *c* is followed by *ie*.

    sufficient   deficient
    efficient

- Generally use *ie* when the sound is a long *e* after any letter except *c*.

    retrieve   piece
    relieve   brief

Spelling Changes When Affixes Are Added

An affix is a syllable added either at the beginning or at the end of a word to change its meaning. The addition of affixes often involves spelling changes.

PREFIXES

A prefix is a syllable added to the beginning of a word. One prefix may be spelled in several different ways, usually depending on the beginning letter of the base word. For example, *com*, *con*, *cor*, and *co* are all spellings of a prefix meaning *together, with*. It is used to form such words as *commit*, *collect*, and *correspond*.

Following are some common prefixes and illustrations showing how they are added to base words. The meaning of the prefix is in parentheses.

ad (to, toward): In adding the prefix *ad* to a base, the *d* often is changed to the same letter as the beginning letter of the base.

    ad + breviate—abbreviate
    ad + commodate—accommodate

com (together, with): The spelling is "com" unless the base word begins with *l* or *r*; then the spelling is *col* and *cor*, respectively.

    com + mit—commit
    com + lect—collect
    com + respond—correspond

de (down, off, away): This prefix is often incorrectly written *di*. Note the correct spellings of words using this prefix.

> describe   desire
> despair   destroyed

dis (apart, from, not): The prefix *dis* is usually added unchanged to the base word.

> dis + trust—distrust
> dis + satisfied—dissatisfied

in (not): The consonant *n* often changes to agree with the beginning letter of the base word.

> in + reverent—irreverent
> in + legible—illegible

> The *n* may change to *m*.

> in + partial—impartial
> in + mortal—immortal

sub (under): This is added unchanged.

> sub + marine—submarine
> sub + let—sublet

un (not): This is added unchanged.

> un + able—unable
> un + fair—unfair

SUFFIXES

A suffix is a syllable added to the end of a word. One suffix may be spelled in several different ways, such as *ance* and *ence*. Also, the base word may require a change in form when a suffix is added. Because of these possibilities, adding suffixes often causes spelling difficulties. Learning the following suffixes and the spelling of the exemplary words will improve your vocabulary and spelling immeasurably. The meaning of the suffix is in parentheses.

able, ible (capable of being): Adding this suffix to a base word, usually a verb or a noun, forms an adjective.

rely—reliable	sense—sensible
consider—considerable	horror—horrible
separate—separable	terror—terrible
read—readable	destruction—destructible
laugh—laughable	reduce—reducible
advise—advisable	digestion—digestible
commend—commendable	comprehension—comprehensible

ance, ence (act, quality, state of): Adding this suffix to a base word, usually a verb, forms a noun.

appear—appearance	exist—existence
resist—resistance	prefer—preference
assist—assistance	insist—insistence
attend—attendance	correspond—correspondence

Other nouns using *ance, ence* include:

ignorance	experience
brilliance	intelligence
significance	audience
importance	convenience
abundance	independence
performance	competence
guidance	conscience

ary, ery (related to, connected with): Adding this suffix to base words forms nouns and adjectives.

boundary	gallery
vocabulary	cemetery
dictionary	millinery
library	
customary	

efy, ify (to make, to become): Adding this suffix forms verbs.

liquefy	ratify
stupefy	testify
rarefy	falsify
putrefy	justify
	classify

ize, ise, yze (to cause to be, to become, to make conform with): These suffixes are verb endings all pronounced the same way.

recognize	revise	analyze
familiarize	advertise	paralyze
generalize	exercise	
emphasize	supervise	
realize		
criticize		
modernize		

Also some nouns end in *ise*.

exercise	enterprise
merchandise	franchise

ly (in a specified manner, like, characteristic of): Adding this suffix to a base noun forms an adjective; adding *ly* to a base adjective forms an adverb. Generally *ly* is added to the base word with no change in spelling.

monthly	surely
accidently	softly
earthly	annually
randomly	clearly

If the base word ends in *ic*, usually you add *ally*.

critically	drastically
basically	automatically

An exception is *public—publicly*.

ous (full of): Adding this suffix to a base noun forms an adjective.

courageous	outrageous	grievous
dangerous	humorous	mischievous
hazardous	advantageous	beauteous
marvelous	adventurous	bounteous

Other suffixes are *ant* (*ent, er, or, ian*) meaning "one who" or "pertaining to"; *ion* (*tion, ation, ment*) meaning "action," "state of," "result"; *ish* meaning "like a"; *less* meaning "without"; and *ship* meaning "skill," "state," "quality," "office."

Final letters of words often require change before certain suffixes can be added.

• Final *e*: A final silent *e* usually is kept before a suffix beginning with a consonant but dropped before a suffix beginning with a vowel (except as noted below).

> write—writing.   use—useful

• Final *ce* and *ge*: Retain the *e* when adding *able* to keep the *c* or *g* soft. If the *e* were dropped, the *c* would have a *k* sound in pronunciation and the *g* a hard *g* sound. For example, the word *change* retains the *ge* when *able* is added: *changeable*.

• Final *ie*: Before adding *ing*, drop the *e* and change the *i* to *y* to avoid doubling the *i*.

> tie—tying   lie—lying

• In adding *ing* to the following words, retain the *e* to avoid confusion with another word.

> dye—dyeing   die—dying
> hoe—hoeing   ho—hoing
> singe—singeing   sing—singing

• Exceptions to the rules above are the following words:

> true—truly   whole—wholly
> due—duly   argue—argument
> judge—judgment (sometimes spelled *judgement*)

• Final *y*. To add suffixes to words ending in a final *y* preceded by a consonant, change the *y* to *i* before adding the suffix. In words ending in *y* preceded by a vowel, the *y* remains unchanged before the suffix.

> survey—surveying   try—tries

• Final consonants. Double the final consonant before adding a suffix beginning with a vowel if:

The word ending in a consonant preceded by a vowel is a one-syllable word:

plan—planned

To add *ed* to *plan*, double the final *n*. Reason: *Plan* is a one-syllable word, it ends in the consonant *n*, the *n* is preceded by the vowel *a*, and the suffix to be added begins with the vowel *e*.

• The word ending in a consonant preceded by a vowel is not stressed on the first syllable:

prefer—preferring—preferred
refer—referring—referred
confer—conferring—conferred
defer—deferring—deferred

• In adding suffixes to some words, the stress shifts from the last syllable of the base word to the first syllable. When the stress is on the first syllable, do *not* double the final consonant.

prefer—preference   confer—conference
refer—reference   defer—deference

CEED, SEDE, CEDE

The base words *ceed*, *sede*, and *cede* sound the same when they are pronounced. However, they cannot correctly be interchanged in spelling.

• *ceed*: Three words, all verbs, end in *ceed*.

proceed   succeed   exceed

• *sede*: The only word ending in *sede* is *supersede*.

• *cede*: All other words, excluding the four named above, ending in this sound are spelled *cede*.

recede   secede   accede
concede   intercede   precede

WORD CHOICE

The English language has an unparalleled richness and diversity in its vocabulary. Thus, to express an idea, you have a wide choice of words to use. To select the words that best convey your intended meaning, you must use denotative and connotative words as needed, choose between specific and general words, and practice conciseness.

Denotation and Connotation

Language could be used more easily and communication would be much simpler if words meant the same things to all people at all times. Unfortunately they do not. Meanings of words shift with the user, the situation, the section of the country, and the context (all the other words surrounding a particular word). Every word has at least two areas of meaning: denotation and connotation.

The denotative meaning is the physical referent the word identifies, the thing or the concept: it is the dictionary definition. Words like *flower, book, shoe, tractor, desk,* and *car* have physical referents; *hope, love, faith, courage, bravery,* and *fear* refer to qualities or concepts.

The connotative meaning of a word is what an individual feels about it because of past experiences in using, hearing, or seeing the word. Each person develops attitudes toward words because certain associations cause the words to suggest qualities either good or bad. For some people, such words as *communist, Red, liberal, leftist, democrat, republican,* or *right-wing* are favorable; for others they are not. The effects of words depend on the emotional reactions and attitudes that the words evoke.

Consider the words *fat, large, portly, obese, plump, corpulent, stout, chubby,* and *fleshy.* Each of these could be used to describe a person's size, some with stronger connotation than others. A girl might not object too much to being described as *plump,* but she might object strongly to being described as *fat.* On the other hand, she probably would not object to receiving a *fat* pay check. Some words may evoke an unfavorable attitude in one context, "*fat* girl," and a favorable attitude in another, "*fat* pay check."

Some words always seem to have pleasant connotations; for example, *truth, success, bravery, happiness, honor, intelligence,* and *beauty.* Other words, such as *lust, hate, spite, insanity, disease, rats, poverty,* and *evil,* usually have unpleasant connotations.

You should choose words that have the right denotation and the desired connotation to clarify your meaning and evoke the response you want from your reader. Compare the following sentences. The first illustrates a kind of writing in which words point to things (denotation) rather than attitudes; the words themselves call for no emotional response, favorable or unfavorable.

> Born in the Fourth Ward with its prevailing environment, John was separated from his working mother when he was one year of age.

The second sentence, through the use of connotative meaning, calls for an emotional response—an unfavorable one.

> Born in the squalor of a Fourth Ward ghetto, John was abandoned by his barroom-entertainer mother while he was still in diapers.

Specific and General Words

A specific word identifies a particular person, object, place, quality, or occurrence; a general word identifies a group or a class. For example, *lieutenant* indicates a person of a particular rank; *officers* indicates a group. For any general word there are numerous specific words; the group identified by *officers* includes such specific terms as *lieutenant*, *general*, *colonel*, and *admiral*.

There are any number of steps or levels as words progress from the general to the more specific:

General	Specific
transportation automobile	Buick Electra
athletes team football team professional football team	Greenbay Packers

The more specific the word choice, the easier for the reader to know exactly the intended meaning.

General	Specific
The gift was expensive.	The alligator billfold cost $49.50.
The bird was in a tree.	The robin was perched on the top-most branch of the cherry tree.
The place was damaged.	The tornado blew out all the windows in the administration building at Midwestern College.

Using general words is much easier, of course, than using specific words; the English language is filled with "umbrella" terms with broad meanings. These words come readily to mind, whereas the specific words that express exact meaning require thought. To write effectively you must search until you find the right words to convey your intended meaning.

Conciseness

In communication, clarity is of primary importance. One way to achieve clarity is to be concise. Conciseness—saying much in a few words—omits nonessential words, uses simple words and direct word patterns, and combines sentence elements. It is important to remember that you can be concise without being brief and that what is short is not necessarily concise. The essential quality in conciseness is making every word count.

OMITTING NONESSENTIAL WORDS

Nonessential words weaken emphasis in a sentence by thoughtlessly repeating an idea or throwing in "deadwood" to fill up space. Note the improved effectiveness in the following sentences when unnecessary words are omitted.

Wordy and needlessly repetitious	Revised
The train arrives at 2:30 p.m. in the afternoon.	The train arrives at 2:30 p.m.
He was inspired by the beautiful character of his surroundings.	He was inspired by his surroundings.
In the event that a rain comes up, close the windows.	If it rains, close the windows.

Eliminating unnecessary words makes writing more exact, more easily understood, and more economical. Often, care in revision will weed out the clutter of deadwood and needless repetition.

SIMPLE WORDS AND DIRECT WORD PATTERNS

An often-told story illustrates quite well the value of simple, unpretentious words stated directly to convey a message. A plumber, having found that hydrochloric acid was good for cleaning out pipes, wrote a government agency about his discovery. The plumber received this reply: "The efficiency of hydrochloric acid is indisputable,

but the corrosive residue is incompatible with metallic permanence."
The plumber responded that he was glad his discovery was helpful.
After several more garbled and misunderstood communications from
the agency, the plumber finally received his clearly stated response:
"Don't use hydrochloric acid. It eats the inside out of pipes." Much
effort and time could have been saved if this had been the wording
of the agency's *first* response.

Generally, use simple words instead of polysyllabic words and
avoid giving too many details in needless modifiers. Compare the
following examples.

Wordy, obscure language	Simple, direct language
Feathered bipeds of similar plumage will live gregariously.	Birds of a feather flock together.
Verbal contact with Mr. Jones regarding the attached notification of promotion has elicited the attached representations intimating that he prefers to decline the assignment.	Mr. Jones does not want the job.
Believing that the newer model air conditioning unit would be more effective in cooling the study area, I am of the opinion that it would be advisable for the community library to purchase a newer model air conditioning unit.	The community library should buy a new air conditioning unit.

COMBINING SENTENCE ELEMENTS

Many sentences are complete and unified yet ineffective because
they lack conciseness. Parts of sentences, or even entire sentences,
often may be reduced or combined.

Study the following examples.

Reducing several words to one word	The registrar *of the college* . . . . The *college* registrar . . . .
Reducing a clause	. . . a house *which is shaped like a cube*.
to a phrase	. . . a house *shaped like a cube*.
or to one word	. . . a *cube-shaped* house.

Reducing a compound sentence	Mendel planted peas for experimental purposes, and from the peas he began to work out the universal laws of heredity.
to a complex sentence	Mendel, as he experimented with peas, began to work out the laws of heredity.
or to a simple sentence	Mendel, experimenting with peas, began to work out the laws of heredity.
Combining two short sentences	Many headaches are caused by emotional tension. Stress also causes a number of headaches.
into one sentence	Many headaches are caused by emotional tension and stress.

Words Often Confused and Misused

Here is a list of often confused and misused words, with suggestions for their proper use.

a, an: *A* is used before words beginning with a consonant sound; *an* is used before words with a vowel sound. (Remember: Consider sound, not spelling.) *Examples*: This is *a* banana. This is *an* orange.

accept, except: *Accept* means "to take an object or idea offered" or "to agree to something"; *except* means "to leave out" or "excluding." *Examples*: Please *accept* this gift. Everyone *except* Joe may leave.

access, excess: *Access* is a noun meaning "way of approach" or "admittance"; *excess* means "greater amount than required or expected." *Examples*: The children were not allowed *access* to the laboratory. His income is in *excess* of fifty thousand dollars.

ad: *Ad* is a shortcut to writing "advertisement." In formal writing, however, write out the full word. In informal writing and speech, such abbreviated forms as *ad*, *auto*, *phone*, *photo*, and *TV* may be acceptable.

advice, advise: *Advice* is a noun meaning "opinion given," "suggestions"; *advise* is a verb meaning "to suggest," "to recommend." *Examples*: We accepted the lawyer's *advice*. The lawyer *advised* us to drop the charges.

affect, effect: *Affect*, as a verb, means "to influence" or "to pretend"; as a noun, it is a psychological term meaning "feeling" or "emotion." *Effect*, as a verb, means "to make something happen"; as a noun, it means "result" or "consequence." *Examples*: Colors used in a home may *affect* the prospective buyer's decision to buy. The new technique will *effect* a change in the entire procedure.

aggravate, irritate: *Aggravate* means "to make worse or more severe." Avoid using *aggravate* to mean "to irritate" or "to vex," except perhaps in informal writing or speech.

ain't: A contraction for "am not," "are not," "has not," "have not." This form is still regarded as substandard; the most careful speakers and writers do not use it.

a lot, alot, allot: *A lot* is written as two separate words and is a colloquial term meaning "a large amount"; *alot* is a common miswriting for "a lot"; *allot* is a verb meaning "to give a certain amount."

all ready, already: *All ready* means that everyone is prepared or that something is completely prepared; *already* means "completed" or "happened earlier." *Examples*: We are *all ready to go*. It is *already* dark.

almost, most: *Almost* is an adverb meaning "nearly"; *most* is an adverb meaning "the greater part of a whole." *Examples*: The emergency shift *almost* froze. The emergency shift worked *most* of the night.

all right, alright: Use *all right*. In time, *alright* may become accepted, but for now *all right* is generally preferred. *Example*: Your choice is *all right* with me.

all together, altogether: *All together* means "united"; *altogether* means "entirely." *Examples*: We will meet *all together* at the clubhouse. There is *altogether* too much noise in the hospital area.

among, between: Use *among* when talking about more than two. Use *between* to express the relation between two things or the relation of a thing to many surrounding things.

amount, number: *Amount* refers to mass or quantity; *number* refers to items, objects, or ideas that can be counted individually. *Examples*: The *amount* of money for clothing is limited. A large *number* of people are enrolled in the class.

angel, angle: *Angel* means "a supernatural being"; *angle* means "corner" or "point of view." Be careful not to overuse *angle* meaning "point of view." Use "point of view," "aspect," etc.

anywheres, somewheres, nowheres: Use *anywhere, somewhere,* or *nowhere.*

as if, like: *As if* is a subordinate conjunction; it should be followed by a subject-verb relationship to form a dependent clause. *Like* is a preposition; in formal writing *like* should be followed by a noun or a pronoun as its object. *Examples*: He reacted to the suggestion *as if* he never heard of it. Pines, *like* cedars, do not have leaves.

as regards, in regard to: Avoid these phrases. Use *about* or *concerning.*

being that, being as how: Avoid using either of these awkward phrases. Use *since* or *because. Example: Because* the bridge is closed, we will have to ride the ferry.

beside, besides: *Beside* means "alongside," "by the side of," or "not part of"; *besides* means "furthermore" or "in addition." *Examples*: The tree stands *beside* the walk. Besides the cost there is a handling charge.

brake, break: *Brake* is a noun meaning "an instrument to stop something"; *break* is a verb meaning "to smash," "to cause to fall apart." *Examples*: The mechanic relined the *brakes* in the truck. If the vase is dropped, it will *break.*

can't hardly: This is a double negative; use *can hardly.*

capital, capitol: *Capital* means "major city of a state or nation," "wealth," or, as an adjective, "chief" or "main." *Capitol* means "building that houses the legislature"; written with a capital "C" it usually means the legislative building in Washington. *Examples*: Jefferson City is the *capital* of Missouri. Our company has a large *capital* investment in preferred stocks. The *capitol* is located on Third Avenue.

cite, sight, site: *Cite* is a verb meaning "to refer to"; *sight* is a noun meaning "view" or "spectacle"; *site* is a noun meaning "location." *Examples*: *Cite* a reference in the text to support your theory. Because of poor *sight*, he has to wear glasses. This is the building *site* for our new home.

coarse, course: *Coarse* is an adjective meaning "rough," "harsh," or "vulgar"; *course* is a noun meaning "a way," "a direction." *Examples*: The sandpaper is too *coarse* for this wood. The creek followed a winding *course* to the river.

consensus: *Consensus* means "a general agreement of opinion." Therefore, do not write "consensus of opinion"; it is repetitious.

contact: *Contact* is overused as a verb, especially in business and industry. Consider using in its place such exact forms as "write to," "telephone," "talk with," "inform," "advise," or "ask."

continual, continuous: *Continual* means "often repeated"; *continuous* means "uninterrupted" or "unbroken." *Examples*: The conference has had *continued* interruptions. The rain fell in a *continuous* downpour for an hour.

could of: The correct form is *could have*. This error occurs because of the sound heard in pronouncing such statements as: We *could have* (could've) completed the work on time.

council, counsel, consul: *Council* is a noun meaning "a group of men appointed or elected to serve in an advisory or legislative capacity." *Counsel*, as a noun, means "advice" or "attorney"; as a verb, it means "to advise." *Consul* is a noun naming the official representing his country in a foreign nation. *Examples*: The club has four members on its *council*. The *counsel* for the defense advised him to testify. The *consul* from Switzerland was invited to our international tea.

device, devise: *Device* is a noun meaning "a contrivance," "an appliance," "a scheme"; *devise* is a verb meaning "to invent." *Examples:* This *device* will help prevent pollution of our waterways. We need to *devise* a safer method for drilling offshore oil wells.

different from, different than: Although *different from* is perhaps more common, *different than* is also an acceptable form.

dual, duel: *Dual* means "double." *Duel* as a noun, means a fight or contest between two people; as a verb, it means "*to fight*." *Examples:* The car has a *dual exhaust*. He was shot in a *duel*.

due to: Some authorities object to *due to* in adverbial phrases. Acceptable substitutes are *owing to* and *because of*.

each and every: Use one or the other. *Each and every* is a wordy way to say "each" or "every." *Example: Each* person should make a contribution.

except for the fact that: Avoid using this wordy and awkward phrase.

fact, the fact that: Use "that."

field: Used too often to refer to an area of knowledge or a subject.

had ought, hadn't ought: Avoid using these phrases. Use *ought* or *should. Example:* He *should not* speak so loudly.

hisself: Use *himself.*

in case, in case of, in case that: Avoid using this overworked phrase. Use *if.*

in many instances: Wordy. Use *frequently* or *often.*

in my estimation, in my opinion: Wordy. Use *I believe* or *I think.*

irregardless: Though you hear this double negative and see it in print, it should be avoided. Use *regardless.*

its, it's: *Its* is the possessive form; *it's* is the contraction for *it is.* The simplest way to avoid confusing these two forms is to think *it is* when writing *it's. Examples:* The tennis team won *its* match. *It's* time for lunch.

lay, lie: *Lay* means "to put down" or "place." Forms are *lay, laid,* and *laying.* It is a transitive verb; thus it denotes action going to an object or to the subject. *Examples*: Lay the books on the table. We *laid* the floor tile yesterday. *Lie* means "to recline" or "rest." Forms are *lie, lay, lain,* and *lying.* It is an intransitive verb; thus it is never followed by a direct object. *Examples*: The pearls *lay* in the velvet-lined case. *Lying* in the velvet-lined case were the pearls.

lend, loan: *Lend* is a verb. *Loan* is used as a noun or a verb; however, many careful writers use it only as a noun.

loose, lose: *Loose* means "to release," "to set free," "unattached," or "not securely fastened"; *lose* means "to suffer a loss." *Examples*: We turned the horses *loose* in the pasture, but we locked the gate so that we wouldn't *lose* them.

lots of, a lot of: In writing use *many, much, a large amount.*

might of, ought to of, must of, would of: *Of* should be *have.* See *could of.*

off of: Omit *of.* Use *off.*

on account of: Use *because*.

one and the same: Wordy. Use *the same*.

outside of: Use *besides, except for,* or *other than*.

passed, past: *Passed* identifies an action and is used as a verb; *past* means "earlier" and is used as a modifier. *Examples*: He *passed* us going eighty miles an hour. In the *past*, bills were sent out each month.

personal, personnel: *Personal* is an adjective meaning "private," "pertaining to the person"; *personnel* is a noun meaning "body of persons employed." *Examples*: Please do not open my *personal* mail. He is is charge of hiring new *personnel*.

plain, plane: *Plain* is an adjective meaning "simple," "without decoration"; *plane* is a noun meaning "airplane," "tool," or "type of surface." *Examples*: The *plain* decor of the room created a pleasing effect. We worked all day checking the *plane's* engine.

principal, principle: *Principal* means "highest," "main," or "head"; *principle* means "belief," "rule of conduct," or "fundamental truth." *Examples*: The school has a new *principal*. His refusal to take a bribe was a matter of *principle*.

proved, proven: Use either form.

put across: Use more exact terms, such as *demonstrate, explain, prove,* or *establish*.

quiet, quite: *Quiet* is an adjective meaning "silence" or "free from noise"; *quite* is an adverb meaning "completely" or "wholly." *Examples*: Please be *quiet* in the library. It's been *quite* a while since I've seen him.

rarely ever, seldom ever: Avoid using these phrases. Use *rarely* or *seldom*.

read where: Use *read that*.

reason is because, reason why: Omit *because* and *why*.

respectfully, respectively: *Respectfully* means "in a respectful manner"; *respectively* means "in the specified order." *Examples*: I *respectfully* explained my objection. The capitals of Libya, Iceland, and Tasmania are Tripoli, Reykjavik, and Hobart, *respectively*.

sense, since: *Sense* means "ability to understand"; *since* is a preposition meaning "until now," an adverb meaning "from then until now," and a conjunction meaning "because." *Examples*: At least he has a *sense* of humor. I have been on duty *since* yesterday.

stationary, stationery: *Stationary* is an adjective meaning "fixed"; *stationery* is a noun meaning "paper used in letter writing." *Examples*: The work bench is *stationary*. The school's *stationery* is purchased through our firm.

state: Use exact terms such as *say, remark, declare, observe*. To *state* means "to declare in a formal statement."

their, there, they're: *Their* is a possessive pronoun; *there* is an adverb of place; *they're* is a contraction for *they are*. *Examples*: *Their* band is in the parade. *There* goes the parade. *They're* in the parade.

this here, that there: Avoid this phrasing. Use *this* or *that*. *Example*: *This* machine is not working properly.

thusly: Use *thus*.

till, until: Either word may be used.

to, too, two: *To* is a preposition; *too* is an adverb telling "how much"; *two* is a numeral.

try and: *Try to* is generally preferred.

type, type of: In writing, use *type of*.

used to could: Use *formerly was able* or *used to be able*.

where . . . at: Omit the *at*. Write, "*Where* is the library?" (not "Where is the library at?")

who's, whose: *Who's* is the contraction for *who is*; *whose* is the possessive form of *who*. *Examples*: *Who's* on the telephone? *Whose* coat is this?

-wise: Currently used and overused as an informal suffix in such words as "timewise," "safetywise," "healthwise." Better to avoid such usage.

would of: The correct form is *would have*. This error occurs because of the sound heard in pronouncing such a statement as this: He *would have* (would've) come if he had not been ill.

7
Grammatical Usage

English-language usage varies and constantly changes. The attempts made to classify language by usage common to dialects (geographical areas), social status, or style (formal and informal usage) are all incomplete and overlapping. However, while there is no such thing as "correct" grammatical usage, there are generally accepted practices.

Usage does make a difference. In writing, select the usage most likely to get the desired results, recognizing that usages, like people, have different characteristics. For example, you write "I have known him a week," rather than "I have knowed him a week," because "I have known him a week" is more acceptable to most people. You base this decision, consciously or unconsciously, on the grammatical expressions of people you respect and the reactions of persons to those expressions.

Because judgments are based on knowledge, the following guides are designed to improve your judgment by increasing your knowledge of acceptable grammatical usages.

PARTS OF SPEECH: DEFINITION AND USAGE

Adjectives

Adjectives describe, limit, or qualify a noun or pronoun by telling "which one?" "what kind?" or "how many?"

Describing adjective	the *gray* paint	tells "what kind?"
Limiting adjective	*three* pencils	tells "how many?"
Qualifying adjective	*younger* sister	tells "which one?"

Adjectives also show degrees of comparison through affixing *-er* and *-est* to the positive form or adding "more" and "most":

Degrees of Comparison

Positive:	tall	beautiful
Comparative:	taller	more beautiful
Superlative:	tallest	most beautiful

The comparative degree is used when speaking of two things and the superlative when speaking of three or more. Short words generally add *-er* and *-est* while longer words require "more" and "most."

The building is *tall*.
The building is *taller* than any other building.
The building is *tallest* of all the buildings.

Be careful not to write a double comparison such as "most beautifulest"; either the *-est* or the *most* makes the superlative degree, not both. Adjectives which indicate absolute qualities or conditions (such as unique, round, or perfect) should not be compared.

Adjectives may be a word, a phrase, or a clause:

The newest structure is a *brick* building.   (Word)
The newest structure is a building *of brick*.   (Phrase)
The newest structure is a building *made of brick*.   (Phrase)
The newest structure is a building *that is made of brick*.
(Clause)

Adjective clauses may be punctuated or not according to the purpose they serve. If they are essential to the meaning of the sentence, they are not set off by commas. If they give additional information, they are set off from the rest of the sentence. Adjective clauses beginning with *that* are always essential and are not set off.

Edward Jenner is the man *who experimented with smallpox vaccination*.   (Clause is essential to meaning)

Bathrooms are often decorated in colors *that suggest water*.
(Clause is essential to meaning)

My ideas about exploration of space, *which are different from most of my friends' ideas*, were formulated mainly through reading.   (Clause gives additional information)

Many different grammatical units may be used as adjectives.

Possessive Pronoun: *My* car is parked in the lot next to the hotel.

Participle: An experience *shared with someone you love* becomes more meaningful.

Infinitive: The course *to be completed* is Sociology 213.

Prepositional Phrase: The man *in the gray suit* is Joe Regal.

Adverbs

Adverbs modify verbs, adjectives, or other adverbs by telling "when?" (time), "where?" (place), "how?" (manner), or "how much?" (degree).

The class began *late*.   (Tells "when?")

The recording session will take place *in Booth A.*   (Tells "where?")

Experts or experienced salesmen can recognize a quality product *by inspection.*   (Tells "how?")

In our laboratories we have containers of *very* clear plastic. (Tells "how much?")

Adverbs may be a word, a phrase, or a clause.

John finished the assignment *effortlessly*.   (Word)

John finished the assignment *with little effort*.   (Phrase)

John finished the assignment *although he exerted little effort*. (Clause)

Many different grammatical units may be used as adverbs.

Prepositional Phrase: Are you going *to the intra-squad game?*

Noun: This income should be reported next *year*.
Infinitive phrase: I came *to see the drill team practice*.

Introductory adverb clauses are separated from the rest of the sentence by a comma.

When a boy asks a girl for a date, he hopes she will accept.

Although most people agree clothes do not make the man, they spend considerable time and money dressing themselves in the latest fashions.

Conjunctions

A conjunction connects words, phrases, or clauses.

Spike, Trim, and *Blair* play in a blues band.   (Words)

We plan to go *to Astroworld, to a baseball game in the Astrodome,* and *on a tour of NASA.*   (Phrases)

The announcement was *that a tornado had been sighted* and *that persons in the area should move to a place of safety.* (Clauses)

There are two classes of conjunctions—coordinating conjunctions and subordinating conjunctions.

Coordinating conjunctions—such as *and, but, or*—connect words, phrases, or clauses of equal rank.

I bought bread, milk, sugar, *and* coffee.   (*And* connects nouns in a series)
Ann *or* Nell will serve on the committee.   (*Or* connects nouns)

Conjunctive adverbs—such as *however, moreover, therefore, consequently, nevertheless*—are also coordinating conjunctions. They link the independent clause in which they occur to the preceding independent clause. The clause they introduce is grammatically independent, but it depends on the preceding clause for complete meaning.

The film was produced and directed by students; other students, *therefore,* should be interested in viewing the film.

Jane had a severe cold; *consequently* she was unable to participate in the bowling tournament.

Correlative conjunctions—*either . . . or, neither . . . nor, both . . . and, not only . . . but also*—are coordinating conjunctions used in pairs to connect words, clauses, and phrases of equal rank.

The movie was *not only* well produced *but also* beautifully filmed.

Be sure that the units joined by correlative conjunctions are the same grammatically.

Incorrect: I *either* will go today *or* tomorrow. (Join verb and adverb).

Revised: I will go either today or tomorrow. (Join adverb and adverb).

Subordinate conjunctions—such as *when, since, because, although, as, as if*—introduce subordinate clauses.

Because Tom was sick, Jim took his place on the first team.

The instructor gave credit for class participation *since the primary purpose of the course was to stimulate thought.*

Nouns

Nouns name persons (Mr. Jones), places (Portland, Oregon), things (tricycle), actions (running), and qualities (mercy).

Nouns can also be characterized by their ability to add an affix to show both possession and plurality.

The *man's* overcoat protected him from the cold. (*Man* has *'s* to form possessive)

Experiences teach vivid *lessons.* (*Experience* and *lesson* add *s* to form plurals)

A word, a phrase, or a clause may function as a noun.

The *record* sold one million *copies.* (Word)

Simon and Garfunkel's "Bridge Over Troubled Water" voices *man's desire to help one another.* (Phrase)

Recording my first record was a unique experience. (Phrase)

The group believed *that the record would be a hit.* (Clause)

Note: The examples of noun phrases and clauses may be analyzed in two ways. Generally, the italicized sections above may be identified simply as noun phrases and noun clauses. More specifically, they may also be analyzed on the basis of elements within them. For example, *Recording my first record* includes *recording*, a gerund used as subject; *my* and *first*, adjectives; *record*, noun used as the object of *recording*.

Nouns have many uses in sentences.

Subject: A noun identifying *who* or *what* the sentence is about.

The *bus* will leave promptly at 3:10 p.m.

Direct Object: A noun identifying *what* or *who* receives the action expressed by the verb.

I enjoy an occasional *dinner* at a Chinese restaurant.

Predicate Noun (Predicate Nominative, Subjective Complement): A noun following a linking verb and referring to the subject of the sentence.

My favorite meal is *steak* and *potatoes*.

Indirect Object: The noun used as an indirect object identifies *to whom* or *for whom* the action expressed by the verb is done. If the *to* or *for* appears in the sentence, the indirect object becomes a prepositional phrase.

Indirect Object: The children gave *Spot* a bath.
They bought *him* a new leash.

Prepositional phrase: They bought a new leash *for him*.

Object of Preposition: The noun following a preposition is the preposition's object.

A trip down the *Ohio River* is a real adventure.

The first step toward competing in the Miss America *pageant* is winning a local contest.

Appositive: The first noun following another noun or pronoun and renaming that noun or pronoun is an appositive.

My gift to John, my oldest *brother,* was cuff links.

We will join my friend *Rose Hamilton.*

Objective Complement: The noun following a direct object, referring to the direct object, and completing its meaning is the
objective complement.

Our YMCA team selected Mark Smith *captain*.

The possessive form of a noun is always used as a modifier.

Flip Wilson's comedy hour is a popular television show.

The *dog's* paw was injured.

Many different grammatical units may be used as nouns.

Gerund and Gerund Phrase: I enjoy *hiking*.   (Direct Object)

Infinitive and Infinitive Phrase: *To view Birmingham at night from
the top of the Vulcan Statue* is a thrilling experience.   (Subject)

Prepositional Phrase: *Over the top* is our goal.   (Subject)

Noun Clause: The spectators realized *that the rain would cause the
game to be canceled.*   (Direct Object)

Prepositions

Traditionally a preposition (such words as *in, by, for, with, at*)
is a word that precedes a noun or a pronoun and shows its relation
to some other word in the sentence, generally a noun, adjective, or
verb. Prepositions are also function words whose forms do not
change; the importance of prepositions lies in their grammatical
function, not in meaning.

A prepositional phrase is composed of the preposition, its object,
and any modifiers between them. It functions as an adjective, adverb,
or noun.

The books *on the shelves* need dusting.   (Adjective)

Most commuting students live *at home*.   (Adverb)

Under the mattress is our hiding place.   (Noun)

Pronouns

A pronoun takes the place of or refers to a noun.

The *women* in the secretarial pool worked overtime.

They worked overtime.

Also, a pronoun is a sub-type of the noun. Through different forms, a pronoun shows possession and plurality and sometimes gender and person. A change in form may also identify the subject and object pronoun.

| he | subject form | *He* is a friend. |
| him | object form | We helped *him*. |

PRONOUN CASE

The personal pronouns and "who" have different forms for different uses in the sentence. These pronoun forms divide into three groups—Nominative Case, Objective Case, and Possessive Case.

Nominative Case Forms

	Singular	Plural
First Person:	I	we
Second Person:	you	you
Third Person:	he, she, it	they
	who, whoever	who, whoever

Nominative case forms may be used as:

Subjects of dependent or independent clauses:

We know about bacteria because of the microscope.

A student hands in an assignment when *it* is completed.

Ferdinand Cohn, *who* was a German botanist, worked out the first scheme for classifying bacteria as plants rather than as animals.

Subjective complements (predicate pronouns) following a form of the verb "to be":

The delegates to the convention are *he* and *I*.

It was *he* who suggested buying the amplifying equipment.

Appositives following a subject or a subjective complement:

> Two students, John and *I*, received awards for achievement.

> The representatives to the convention are students, John and *I*.

Objective Case Forms

	Singular	Plural
First Person:	me	us
Second Person:	you	you
Third Person:	her, him, it	them
	whom, whomever	whom, whomever

Objective case forms may be used as:

Direct object of a verb or of a verbal (infinitive, participle, gerund):

> The flying chips hit *me* in the face.   (Object of verb "hit.")
> The artist carefully handled the clay, shaping *it* so that it did not crack.   (Object of verbal "shaping.")

Indirect objects:

> Give *us* your suggestions.

> The stewardess told *them* the reason for the change in plans.

Objects of prepositions:

> Students like John and *him* will make excellent workers.

> No one but *you* could explain the operation.

> Many students obtain summer work with *them*.

Subjects of infinitives:

> I believe *him* to be the best choice.

> Let *me* help Tom.

Appositives:

> We gave the article to the editors, James and *him*.

Possessive Case Forms

	Singular	Plural
First Person:	my, mine	our, ours
Second Person:	your, yours	your, yours
Third Person:	his, her, hers, its	their, theirs
	whose, whosever	whose, whosever

Possessive pronoun forms are used to:

Show ownership or possession:

Pasteur was also experimenting while Koch and *his* disciples were busy perfecting new techniques.

My choice of warm colors for decorating the bedroom may differ from *your* choice.

Whose guitar is this?

Modify gerunds:

What do you think of *his* finding a more economical way to build the annex?

Proud of *his* becoming the new national chairman, John's friends honored him with a reception.

COMPOUND PRONOUN FORMS WITH "SELF"

Compound personal pronouns are formed by combining the possessive case pronoun forms with -*self* or -*selves*: *myself, yourself, herself, himself, itself, ourselves, yourselves,* and *themselves.*

The compound personal pronouns may be used:

For emphasis, with the pronoun usually following the word emphasized:

My father *himself* ordered those present to be quiet.

I explained the situation to the coach *himself.*

As an object following the verb or a preposition and reflexively referring to the subject:

Did you hurt *yourself?*

He was angry with *himself.*

Avoid using *myself* in the place of *I* or *me.* Never use *themself, theirselves,* and *hisself;* they are not acceptable forms.

WHO AND WHOM

Problems may arise in the use of *who* and *whom.* While *who* can be used in conversation for all purposes, *who* is the nominative case pronoun form and *whom* is the objective case form.

Who delivered the message?   (Subject)

For *whom* was the message left?   (Object of preposition)

Study the following constructions involving *who* and *whom* (*whoever* and *whomever*).

Following a preposition:

To *whom* did the superintendent give the assignment?   (Object of preposition)

The superintendent will give the assignment to *whoever* is qualified. (Subject of verb *is qualified.* The whole clause, *whoever is qualified,* is object of the preposition.)

Unimportant clause separating *who* or *whoever* as subject from verb:

He is the student *who* they say will win the election. (Subject of verb *will win. They say* is an unimportant clause that does not change the subject-verb relationship: *who . . . will win.*)

Verbs

Verbs indicate state of being or express action. For example, in the sentence, "That machine *is* a very expensive piece of equipment," the verb *is* indicates state of being. In the sentence, "The authority on the prevention of water pollution *studied* the city's water problem carefully," *studied* expresses action.

Verbs have several characteristics which require changes in the form of the verbs. These characteristics are tense, mood, voice, person, and number. Person and number, which affect subject-verb agreement, are discussed on pages 172–175.

Verb tense indicates the time of the state of being or action. This important characteristic establishes whether the action stated by the verb *has* already happened, *is* happening now, or *will* happen in the future. For example, if you heard or read "I went to work," you would know without any conscious effort that the action had already taken place. If the statement were "I enjoy work," you would know that the action is going on in the present. Finally, with "I shall go to work," you know that the action will take place in the future. Verb tenses then are crucial to meaning.

The three simple tenses are present, past, and future:

Present tense verbs indicate action taking place now, or continuing action.

I *work* eight hours a day.

Past tense verbs indicate action completed before the present time.

I *worked* ten hours a day on my previous job.

Future tense verbs indicate action that will occur at some time in the future, some time after the present.

I *will work* eight hours a day beginning November 1.

The three more complex tenses are present perfect, past perfect, and future perfect:

Present perfect tense verbs indicate action completed prior to the present or action begun in the past and continuing in the present.

I *have worked* eight hours a day since last spring.

Past perfect tense verbs indicate action completed prior to some stated past time.

I *had worked* eight hours a day until last week when I changed to a new work schedule.

Future perfect tense verbs indicate action to be completed prior to some stated future time.

On June 30 I *will have worked* eight hours a day for thirty straight days.

Verbs also have a form known as the progressive. This can be used with all tenses to show action going on at the present time.

I *am working* eight hours a day.

Formation of Tenses

Verb tenses are formed according to the following formula. Verbs have three principal parts: the present tense (1st principal part—*see*), the past tense (2nd principal part—*saw*), and the past participle (3rd principal part—*seen*). With these three principal parts, various "helping" verbs, and first, second, and third person pronouns, the tenses are formed.

Present Tense:	Pronouns + 1st principal part (add *s* to third person singular form)
Past Tense:	Pronouns + 2nd principal part
Future Tense:	Pronouns + "shall" with first person and "will" with second and third persons + 1st principal part
Present Perfect:	Pronouns + "have" + 3rd principal part (Change "have" to "has" in third person singular)
Past Perfect:	Pronouns + "had" + 3rd principal part
Future Perfect:	Pronouns + "shall" with first person and "will" with second and third persons + "have" + 3rd principal part

The formula above gives active voice verb forms. Passive voice verbs are formed by writing the correct form of the verb "to be" and adding the 3rd principal part of the main verb.

Shifts in Tense

Verb tenses tell the reader when the action is happening. Therefore, avoid needlessly shifting from one tense to another because shifts in tense can confuse the reader.

Shifted verbs: As time *passed*, technology *becomes* more complex.

> *passed*—past tense verb
> *becomes*—present tense verb

> Since the two indicated actions occur at the same time, the verbs should be the same tense.

Consistent verbs: As time *passes*, technology *becomes* more complex.

> *passes*
> *becomes* —present tense

Shifted verbs: I *have been installing* appliances this summer, and I *found* the work difficult but interesting.

> *have been installing*—present perfect progressive
> *found*—past tense

> The verb phrase "have been installing" indicates an action in progress while the verb *found* indicates an action already completed. To indicate that both actions are still in progress, the sentence might be written as follows:

Consistent verbs: I *have been installing* appliances this summer, and I *find* the work difficult but interesting.

> *have been installing*—present perfect progressive
> *find*—present

> Or if both actions have been completed:

Consistent verbs: I *installed* appliances this summer, and I *found* the work difficult but interesting.

> *installed*
> *found* —past tense

MOOD

Verbs have three moods—the indicative, the subjunctive, and the imperative.

The indicative mood, the one most commonly used, makes a statement or asks a question.

Physics is the science of matter and energy.

What is geriatrics?

The subjunctive mood is used to express a condition contrary to fact, a wish, a doubt, or uncertainty.

I wish that I were in line for the promotion.

If I were the instructor, I would require all assigned work on time.

The imperative mood is used to express a command or a request.

Explain the formula used to convert Centigrade to Fahrenheit.

Begin the test.

VOICE

Verbs have two voices, active and passive:

The active voice indicates action done by the subject.

A truck's engine supplies the forward force.

Meat slightly marbled with fat tastes better.

The girl sings.

The passive voice indicates action done to the subject. This verb is always at least two words, a form of the verb "to be" and the past participle (3rd principal part) of the main verb.

Logarithm tables are found on page 210.

Although the active voice has more emphasis than the passive, you will probably find occasions when the passive voice better serves your purpose.

Avoid shifting from the active to the passive voice.

Shift in voice: First *remove* the old paint; then the stain *can be applied.*
remove—active voice
can be applied—passive voice

Consistent voice: First *remove* the old paint; then *apply* the stain.

$$\frac{remove}{apply} \text{—active voice}$$

Shift in voice: Management and labor representatives *discussed* the pay raise, but no decision *was reached*.

> *discussed*—active voice
> *was reached*—passive voice

Consistent voice: Management and labor representatives *discussed* the pay raise, but they *reached* no decision.

$$\frac{discussed}{reached} \text{—active voice}$$

TRANSITIVE AND INTRANSITIVE VERBS

Verbs may be divided into two groups—transitive verbs and intransitive verbs.

Transitive verbs indicate action done by the subject to the object or action done to the subject. If the subject acts, the verb is transitive active; if the subject is acted upon, the verb is transitive passive.

> Before trying a recipe, the cook *should assemble* all needed ingredients, properly measured.   (Subject acting; verb transitive active)

> The term paper *was written* in pencil.   (Subject acted upon; verb transitive passive)

Verbs that have no action going to an object or to a subject are intransitive. Intransitive verbs may be either complete or linking. Complete verbs may be followed by an adverb modifier but not by an adjective modifier or an object.

> The machines *run* continuously.

> The commuters *have left*.

Intransitive linking verbs connect the subject to the complement.

> The food *smelled* good.

> The best light for reading *is* natural north light.

> Some students *are* more energetic than others.

Mr. Overstreet's favorite colors for kitchens *are* yellow and white.

REGULAR AND IRREGULAR VERBS

According to the way they form their principal parts, verbs are divided into two groups—regular (weak) verbs and irregular (strong) verbs.

Regular verbs form the second and third principal parts by adding *-ed* or *-d* to the present form.

Present	Past	Past Participle
walk	walked	walked
plan	planned	planned

A few regular verbs add *-t* to form the second and third principal parts.

keep	kept	kept
build	built	built

The spelling of irregular verbs changes considerably in the forming of the second and third principal parts.

go	went	gone
see	saw	seen
do	did	done
run	ran	run

Verbals

Verbals, either as single words or within phrases, are formed from verbs and used as modifiers or naming words.

> *Singing with a band* is my favorite activity. (Naming)

> *Delegating authority* is a simple and natural process. (Naming)

> The trees *planted on the slope* have prevented further erosion. (Modifier)

Verbals can be divided into three groups—participles, gerunds, and infinitives.

Participles function as adjectives and they have three forms:

present participle (ends in -*ing*), past participle (usually ends in -*ed* or -*en*), and present perfect participle (*having* plus the past participle).

> Pictures *produced by colored light* may replace painted pictures in future twentieth-century homes.

> *Having completed the experiment,* I was convinced that silver was a better conductor than copper.

> *Designing his own home,* the architect used an ultramodern decor.

Participles that are not necessary to identify the word modified are set off in commas. Participles that identify the noun modified are *not* set off in commas.

> Mr. Owens, *presiding at the council meeting,* called for the committee's report.

> A picture *improperly mounted and insecurely fastened* may come loose from the mounting and fall to the floor.

Participles introducing a sentence are set off by a comma.

> *Representing the company,* the salesmen can make contracts.

Gerunds always end in -*ing* and function as nouns.

> *Careful measuring of the pattern* is necessary for proper fit.
> Robert Southwell uses most of his time for *writing reports to be presented to the board.*

Infinitives function as nouns, adjectives, or adverbs, depending on their use in a sentence. There are two forms of the infinitive: present ("to" plus 1st principal part of main verb) and present perfect ("to" plus "have" plus the 3rd principal part of the main verb).

> My purpose is *to become involved in ecological discussions.* (Noun)

> By the first of the year I hope *to have completed the tests.* (Noun)

> This is the equipment *to be returned.* (Adjective)

> *To prevent injury to the worker or damage to materials,* ᵴafe
> practice must be observed at all times.   (Adverb)

Remember that introductory infinitive phrases used as modifiers are
set off by a comma.

> *To secure the most satisfactory results,* buy a good quality
> material.

> *To explain an unfamiliar object,* compare it to a familiar ob-
> ject.

PROBLEMS OF USAGE

Agreement of Pronoun and Antecedent

Pronouns take the place of or refer to nouns. They provide a
good way to economize in writing. For example, writing a paper on
Anthony van Leeuwenhoek's pioneer work in developing micro-
scopes, you could use the pronoun forms *he, his,* and *him* to refer
to Leeuwenhoek rather than repeating his name numerous times.

Since pronouns take the place of or refer to nouns, there must
be number and gender agreement between the pronoun and its antecedent (the word the pronoun stands for or refers to).

AGREEMENT IN NUMBER

A singular antecedent requires a singular pronoun; a plural
antecedent requires a plural pronoun.

> An analysis of a *room* is the first factor in making a color
> scheme for *it.*   (Antecedent *room* and Pronoun *it* both singu-
> lar)

> Drawing *instruments* are generally sold as a set, but *they* may
> be purchased separately.   (Antecedent *instruments* and Pro-
> noun *they* both plural)

> Gritty ink *erasers* should be avoided because *they* invariably
> damage the working surface of the paper.   (Antecedent
> *erasers* and Pronoun *they* both plural)

Study the following constructions involving number agreement
of pronoun and antecedent.

Compound Subjects

Two or more subjects joined by *and* must be referred to by a plural pronoun.

> The *business manager and* the *accountant* plan their budget.

> The *instructor and* the *assistant* will be asked to give *their* reasons for requesting new equipment.

Two or more singular subjects joined by *or* or *nor* must be referred to by singular pronouns.

> The *secretary or* the switchboard *operator* has left *her* purse.

> Neither *Mr. Conway nor Mr. Freeman* will appear to give *his* report.

Collective Nouns

Words identifying a group are called collective nouns—*class, team, committee, band.* When identifying a single unit, such words are referred to by a singular pronoun; when regarded as identifying individual members within a group, such words are referred to by a plural pronoun.

> The *class* submitted *its* project for the semester, a scale model of a three-story building. (Class as a unit prepared one project, singular; Pronoun *its*, singular)

> The *class* submitted *their* semester projects, scale models of houses they had designed. (Individual members each prepared a project, plural; Pronoun *their*, plural)

Such nouns as *part, rest*, and *remainder* may also be singular or plural. The number is determined by a phrase following the noun.

> The remainder of the *students* asked that *their* grades be mailed.

> The rest of the *coffee* was stored in *its* own container.

Indefinite Pronouns

Indefinite pronouns are less exact than other pronouns; their antecedents are not specific persons, places, or things. Some indefinite pronouns are: *each, every, everyone* and *everybody, nobody, either, neither, one, anyone,* and *anybody,* and *someone* and *somebody.* These forms are singular; pronouns referring to them should be singular.

> *Every room* has *its* own peculiarities which affect the solution of *its* color problem.

> *Any* man willing to work can feel secure in *his* job.

> *Neither* of the machines has *its* motor repaired.

The indefinite pronouns *both, many, several,* and *few* are plural; these forms require plural pronouns.

> *Several* realized *their* failure was the result of not studying.

> *Both* felt that nothing could save *them.*

Still other indefinite pronouns—*most, some, all, none, any,* and *more*—may be either singular or plural. Usually a phrase following the indefinite pronoun will reveal whether the pronoun is singular or plural in meaning.

> *Most* of the *patients* were complimentary of *their* nurses.

> *Most* of the *money* was returned to *its* owner.

AGREEMENT IN GENDER

Gender indicates the sex of an object. There are three genders: masculine (male), feminine (female), and neuter (without sex). Some words may have either masculine or feminine gender. For example, *him* is a masculine form; *her* is feminine; *desk* is neuter, *child* is either sex.

A masculine antecedent requires a masculine pronoun form.

> *Mr. Arthur Harvey,* a well-known after dinner speaker, entertained the audience with *his* quick wit.

A feminine antecedent requires a feminine pronoun form.

> Selected as manager of hospital food service, *Mrs. Walker* received *her* training at Walter Reed Hospital.

A neuter antecedent requires a neuter pronoun.

> Since we did not receive all the parts of the *speaker system, it* could not be installed on time.

When referring to people, use the pronouns *who* or *that;* when referring to animals or things, use the pronouns *that* or *which.*

The *supplies that* were purchased in April were shipped within two weeks.

The personnel director must hire *men who* have the skills needed to perform satisfactorily on the job.

SHIFTS IN PERSON

Avoid shifting from one person to another, from one number to another, or from one gender to another because such shifting creates awkward constructions.

Shift in person: When *I* was just an apprentice welder, the boss expected *you* to know all the welding processes.
(*I* is first person; *you* is second person.)
Correction: When *I* was just an apprentice welder, the boss expected *me* to know all the welding processes.
Shift in number: *Each* man in the space center control room watched *his* dial anxiously. *They* thought the countdown to "0" would never come.
(*Each* and *his* are singular pronouns; *They* is plural.)
Correction: *Each* man in the space center control room watched *his* dial anxiously and thought the countdown to "0" would never come.
Shift in gender: The mewing of my cat told me *it* was hungry, so I gave *her* some food.
(*It* is neuter; *her* is feminine.)
Correction: The mewing of my cat told me *she* was hungry, so I gave *her* some food.

Agreement of Subject and Verb

A subject and verb agree in person and number. The following statements and examples should help solve problems in subject-verb agreement.

Person denotes person speaking (1st person), person spoken to (2nd person), and person spoken of (3rd person). The person used determines the verb form that follows. In person agreement there is one exception to the fact that all verb forms within a tense are the same for 1st, 2nd, and 3rd persons, both singular and plural. This exception is 3rd person singular, present tense, indicative mood, which adds "s" or "es" to the first principal part.

Present Tense

1st person	I go	we go
2nd person	you go	you go
3rd person	he goes	they go

• A subject and verb agree in number; that is, a plural subject requires a plural verb and a singular subject requires a singular verb.

The *symbol* for Hydrogen *is* H.   (Singular subject; Singular verb)

Comic *strips are* often vignettes of real life situations.   (Plural subject; Plural verb)

• A compound subject requires a plural verb.

Students and *instructors work* together to formulate policies.

• The pronoun *you* as subject always takes a plural verb.

You were assigned the duties of staff nurse on fourth floor.

• In a sentence containing both a positive and a negative subject, the verb agrees with the positive.

The *employees*, not the manager, *were* asked to give their opinions regarding working conditions.

• Two singular subjects joined by *or* or *nor* take a singular verb. If the two subjects joined by *or* or *nor* are of different numbers (one singular and one plural), the verb agrees with the nearer subject.

A *graph* or a *diagram aids* the interpretation of statistical reports.   (Both subjects singular; Verb singular)
A *graph* or *diagrams aid* the interpretation of this statistical report.   (Subject nearer verb plural; Verb plural)

• A word that is plural in form but names a single object or idea requires a singular verb.

The *United States has changed* from an agricultural economy to a technical economy.

Twenty-five *dollars was offered* any employee who made a usable suggestion for advertising.

Six *inches is* the length of the narrow rule.

• *The number* generally takes a singular verb; *a number* takes a plural verb.

The number of movies attended each year by the average American *has decreased.*

A *number* of modern inventions *are* the product of the accumulation of vast storehouses of smaller, minor discoveries.

• When followed by an *of* phrase, *all, more, most, some,* and *part*; fractions; and percents take a singular verb if the object of the *of* is singular and a plural verb if the object of the *of* is plural.

Two-thirds of his *discussion was* irrelevant.   (Object of *of* phrase "discussion" is singular; Verb singular)

Some of the *problems* in a college environment *require* careful analysis by both faculty and students.   (Object of *of* phrase "problems" is plural; verb plural)

• Elements which come between the subject and the verb ordinarily do not affect subject-verb agreement.

One of the numbers *is* difficult to represent because of the great number of zeroes necessary.

Such *factors* as temperature, available food, age of organism, and nature of the suspending medium *influence* the swimming speed of a given organism.

Occasionally the subject may follow the verb, especially in sentences beginning with *there*; however, such word order does not change the subject-verb agreement.

There *are* many *types* of media that can be used in teaching.

There *are* two common temperature *scales*: Fahrenheit and Centigrade.

There *is* a great *deal* of difference in the counseling techniques used by contemporary ministers.

- Indefinite pronouns (*either, neither, nobody, nothing, each, one, everyone, everybody,* etc.) require singular verbs.

Each of the students in composition *completes* ten themes per semester.

One of the first decisions to be made in furnishing a room or a house *is* the selection of the furniture wood or woods.

Other indefinite pronouns (*all, some, more, most, any,* and *none*) may require singular or plural verbs, depending on whether the phrase following the pronoun in a sentence identifies the pronoun as singular or plural.

Most of the city's *hotels have* convention space for several hundred people. (*Most* is plural because of *hotels;* Verb plural)

Most of the committee's time *has been spent* in discussion. (*Most* is singular because of *time;* Verb singular)

- Collective nouns, words such as *class, team, committee,* naming a group, require a singular verb if the group indicated is regarded as a unit; they require a plural verb when the individual members in the group are indicated.

The *class completes* a project each week.   (Class as a unit or group completes a single project)

The *class complete* their weekly projects each Friday.   (Individual members of class each complete a weekly project)

- Relative pronouns (*who, whom, whose, which, that*) may require a singular or a plural verb, depending on the antecedent of the relative pronoun.

Art structure *elements, which are* basic in all the visual arts, are line, form, color, and texture. (Antecedent of *which* is *elements,* a plural form; Verb plural)

The *Kelly Girl, who is,* as a rule, proficient in all aspects of secretarial work, helps businesses during rush periods.   (Antecedent of *who* is *Kelly Girl,* a singular form; Verb singular)

Modifiers

Modifiers are words, phrases, or clauses, either adjective or adverb, that limit or restrict other words in the sentence. Careless construction and placement of these modifiers may cause problems such as dangling modifiers, dangling elliptical clauses, misplaced modifiers, and squinting modifiers.

DANGLING MODIFIERS

Dangling modifiers or dangling phrases occur when the word the phrase should modify is hidden within the sentence or is missing.

- Word hidden in sentence:

"Holding the bat tightly, the ball was hit by the boy."

Because of the phrase "holding the bat tightly," the subject of the sentence logically would be "boy," yet it is hidden as object of the preposition and the introductory phrase "dangles." The phrase cannot sensibly modify *ball;* certainly it wasn't the ball holding the bat tightly. Correctly stated, the sentence would be arranged as follows: "Holding the bat tightly, the boy hit the ball."

- Word missing: The most common dangling modifier is the verbal phrase at the beginning of the sentence. Correctly used, this phrase relates to the subject of the sentence.

> *Example showing correct use:* By placing a thermometer under the tongue for approximately three minutes, anyone can tell if he has fever. (Phrase "By placing . . . three minutes" correctly refers to "anyone," the subject)

Incorrectly used, the following phrase "dangles:"

> *Example showing incorrect use:* Planning and carrying out the experiment, the theory that opposite charges attract was proved. (Phrase "Planning . . . experiment" incorrectly refers to "theory")

To correct dangling verbal phrases:

Rewrite the sentence so that the word the phrase modifies immediately follows the phrase. (This word usually is the subject of the sentence.)

Planning and carrying out the experiment, the *students* proved that opposite charges attract.   (Phrase "Planning . . . experiment" correctly refers to "students," the subject)

Rewrite the sentence changing the phrase to a dependent clause.

(After the students had planned and carried out the experiment), they accepted the theory that opposite charges attract.

As a test, try reading the introductory phrase after the subject. Is the meaning logical? If so, the sentence structure should be correct.

DANGLING ELLIPTICAL CLAUSES

In elliptical clauses some words are understood rather than stated. For example, the dependent clause in the following sentence is elliptical: When measuring the temperature of a conductor, you must use the Centigrade scale. In the elliptical clause "When measuring . . . conductor," the subject and part of the verb have been omitted. The understood subject of an elliptical clause is the same as the subject of the sentence. In the example this is true: When (you are) measuring the temperature of a conductor, you must use the Centigrade scale. If the understood subject of the elliptical clause is not the same as the subject of the sentence, the clause is a dangling clause.

> *Example showing incorrect use:*   After changing the starter switch, the car still would not start. Certainly it is illogical to say, "After the car changed the starter switch." The sentence must be revised in some way to correct it.

Dangling elliptical clauses may be corrected by:

• Including within the clause the missing words.

> After *the mechanic* changed the starter switch, the car still would not start.

• Rewriting the main sentence so that the stated subject of the sentence and the understood subject of the clause will be the same.

> After changing the starter switch, the *mechanic* still could not start the car.

MISPLACED MODIFIERS

Place modifiers near the word or words modified. If the modifier is correctly placed, there should be no confusion. If the modifier is incorrectly placed, the intended meaning of the sentence may not be clear.

Example of misplaced modifier: The machinist placed the work to be machined in the drill press vise *called the workpiece.*

Correctly placed modifier: The machinist placed the work to be machined, *called the workpiece,* in the drill press vise.

Example of misplaced modifier: The dietitian checked the week's food order *with a frown.*

Correctly placed modifier: The dietitian, *with a frown,* checked the week's food order.

SQUINTING MODIFIERS

A modifier should clearly limit or restrict *one* sentence element. If a modifier is so placed within a sentence that it can be taken to limit or restrict either of two elements, the modifier is squinting; that is, the reader cannot tell which way the modifier is looking.

Example of squinting modifier: When the student began summer work *for the first time* he was expected to follow orders promptly and exactly.

In the sentence the phrase "for the first time" could belong to the introductory clause, "When the student began summer work for the first time," or it could belong to the independent clause, "for the first time he was expected to follow orders promptly and exactly." Punctuation may solve the problem. The sentence might be written in either of the following ways, depending on the meaning intended.

When the student began summer work *for the first time,* he was expected to follow orders promptly and exactly.

When the student began summer work, *for the first time* he was expected to follow orders promptly and exactly.

For another example of a squinting modifier, consider this sentence.

The students were advised *when it was mid-morning* the new class schedule would go into effect.

The squinting modifier "when it was mid-morning" could tell when they were advised or when the new class schedule would go into effect.

The sentence could be rewritten in one of two ways, depending on the meaning intended.

> *When it was mid-morning,* the students were advised that the new class schedule would go into effect.

> The students were advised that the new class schedule would go into effect *when it was mid-morning.*

Particularly difficult for some writers is the correct placement of *only, almost,* and *nearly.* These words generally should be placed immediately before the word they modify, since changing position of these words within a sentence changes the meaning of the sentence.

> In the reorganization of the district the congressman *nearly* lost a hundred voters.   (Didn't lose any voters)

> In the reorganization of the district the congressman lost *nearly* a hundred voters.   (Lost almost one hundred voters)

PARALLELISM IN SENTENCES

Parallel structure involves getting like ideas into like constructions. A coordinate conjunction joins ideas that must be stated in the same grammatical form. For example, an adjective should be parallel with an adjective, a verb with a verb, an adverb clause with an adverb clause, and an infinitive phrase with an infinitive phrase. The parallel in grammar helps to make clear the parallel in meaning.

> A *typewriter,* a *table,* and a *filing cabinet* were delivered today.   (Nouns in parallel structure)

> *Whether you accept the outcome of the experiment* or *whether I accept it* depends on our individual interpretation of the facts.   (Dependent clauses in parallel structure)

Failure to express each of the ideas in the same grammatical form results in faulty parallelism.

> This study should help the future wife *learn* skills and *to be*

knowledgeable about sewing and cooking. (Verb and infinitive phrase)

Revised: This study should help the future wife *learn* skills and *become* knowledgeable about sewing and cooking. (Verbs in parallel structure)

Three qualities of tungsten steel alloys are *strength, ductility,* and *they have to be tough.* (Noun, noun, and independent clause)

Revised: Three qualities of tungsten steel alloys are *strength, ductility,* and *toughness.* (Nouns in parallel structure)

The best lighting in a study room can be obtained *if windows are placed on the north side, if tables are placed so that the light comes over the student's left shoulder,* and *by painting the ceiling a very light color.*   (Dependent clause, dependent clause, phrase)

Revised: The best lighting in a study room can be obtained *if windows are placed on the north side, if tables are placed so that the light comes over the student's left shoulder,* and *if the ceiling is painted a very light color.* (Dependent clauses in parallel structure)

Prepositions

A preposition may end a sentence when any other placement of the preposition would result in a clumsy, unnatural sentence.

Natural: Sex is a topic which many people think *about.*
Unnatural: Sex is a topic *about* which many people think.

Sometimes the so-called preposition functions as an adverb which helps to complete the meaning of the verb.

We will work that *out.*

Everyone was surprised when he walked *in.*

All assignments should be handed *in* by Thursday.

SENTENCE FRAGMENTS

A group of words containing a subject and a verb and standing alone as an independent group of words is a sentence. If a group of words lacks a subject or a verb or cannot stand alone as an independent group of words, it is called a sentence fragment.

Sentence fragments generally occur because:

• A noun (subject) followed by a dependent clause or phrase is written as a sentence. The omitted unit is the verb.

> *Fragment:* The engineer's scale, which is graduated in the decimal system.

> *Fragment:* Colors that are opposite.

To make the sentence fragment into an acceptable sentence, add the verb and any modifiers needed to complete the meaning.

> *Sentence:* The engineer's scale, which is graduated in the decimal system, is often called the decimal scale.

> *Sentence:* Colors that are opposite on the color circle are used in a complementary color scheme.

• Dependent clauses or phrases are written as complete sentences. These are introductory clauses and phrases which require an independent clause.

> *Fragment:* While some pencil tracings are made from a drawing placed underneath the tracing paper.

> *Fragment:* Another development that has promoted the recognition of management.

To make the fragments into sentences, add the independent clause.

> *Sentence:* While some pencil tracings are made from a drawing placed underneath the tracing paper, most drawings today are made directly on pencil tracing paper, cloth, vellum, or bond paper.

Sentence: Another development that has promoted the recognition of management is the separation of ownership and management.

There are occasions when types of fragments are acceptable:

- A sentence with an understood subject.

  In making a drawing directly on tracing paper or cloth, place a stiff, smooth sheet of heavy, white paper underneath. (Understood subject: *You*)

- Transition between ideas in a paragraph or composition.

  Now to the next point to be discussed.

- Dialogue.

  "How many different meals have been planned for next month?" "About ten."

8

The Library Paper

This is a general guide for writing a library paper. It does not attempt to deal with the more intricate points in library research, nor does it attempt to present every acceptable method and form involved in writing a library paper. (The suggested bibliographical and footnote forms are in accordance with *The MLA Style Sheet*, 2nd ed. New York: Modern Language Association, 1970.) This guide does, however, present in a logical, step-by-step sequence a procedure for writing a successful paper. Once you master the basic skills in this procedure, you will have the foundation to advance to even the most difficult library-research problems.

The procedure for writing a library paper centers around four major steps:

1. Selecting a subject and defining the problem.

2. Finding the facts.

3. Recording and organizing the facts.

4. Reporting the facts.

STEP I. SELECTING A SUBJECT AND DEFINING THE PROBLEM

Selecting a Subject

The success of the research project depends on a wise choice of subject. If a specific subject is assigned to you, the selection problem is solved. However, if you choose the subject, several guidelines should be observed.

1. *Choose a subject that is interesting.* Doing research should not be a chore or just another assignment; it should be a pleasant adventure. Investigating some aspect of a future vocation, following up a question or a statement discussed in class, finding out more about an invention or a discovery, wanting to know more about a particular writer or thinker—whatever the subject, let it be something that is really interesting.

2. *Choose a subject that can be treated satisfactorily in the allotted time.* No one expects a college student to make an earth-shaking contribution to human knowledge by presenting the result of months and years of research and study. You do library research to gain experience in finding, organizing, and reporting information on a specific subject. Therefore, choose a topic that is sufficiently limited for adequate treatment in the few weeks allotted for the paper. (For a detailed discussion of selecting and limiting a subject, see pages 49–51 and 74–75.

3. *Choose a subject on which there is sufficient available material.* Before deciding definitely on a subject, check with instructors and the library to be sure that the topic has sufficient accessible material. Generally, it is wise to choose another topic if the principal library you use has little or no information on the proposed topic. (Do not be misled, however, by a *false* survey of available material). If the topic is highly specialized or has information in only very select journals, locate several references before deciding definitely to use the topic. Sometimes a news broadcast or a current event may suggest a subject. Again, be sure that enough material can be secured to write an effective paper.

Defining the General Problem

After selecting the subject for the library paper, the central problem or idea being investigated should be specifically stated. The formulation of this central problem, or basic question, is important, because it determines what information you will gather. In writing a paper, the purpose is not simply to gather information that happens to fall under a general heading. The information must relate directly to the subject and give it form and meaning. For the subject "The Effects of Alcohol on Man," for example, the central problem might be defined as: "How does alcohol affect a person: how does it affect his body, his behavior, and his relationships with other people?" This question gives direction to your reading and to your investigation as a whole.

Defining the Specific Problems

Before starting any research, divide the central problem into specific problems, or questions. These questions serve as a preliminary outline for more selective reading. Again, take the subject, "The Effects of Alcohol on Man" with the central problem, "How does alcohol affect a person: how does it affect his body, his behavior, and his relationships with other people?" Divide this general question into smaller ones, such as these:

1. Does alcohol kill brain cells?

2. Why do people drink?

3. Why do some people become silly and giggle, while others become morose and withdrawn when they drink?

4. What organs of the body does alcohol affect?

5. How does excessive drinking affect family relationships?

6. How much alcohol does it take to have an effect on the body?

7. Why can some people take or leave alcohol while others become addicted to it?

Other questions, of course, might be added to these.

As the investigation proceeds and the body of collected data increases, change, drop, or add to the questions in the preliminary outline.

STEP II. FINDING THE FACTS

After selecting the subject and defining the problem under investigation, you begin the second step in writing a library paper—finding the facts. The various sources of information can be classified as:

1. Personal observation, or experience.

2. Personal interviews.

3. Free or inexpensive materials from various agencies.

4. Library materials.

From these general sources, compile a list of specific sources—books, periodicals, people, agencies, companies—that could supply the information you want.

Personal Observation, or Experience

Personal observation, or experience, often makes your writing more realistic and vivid; and sometimes this observation or experience is essential. If you were writing, for instance, about the need for more up-to-date mental-care facilities in your state, personal inspections would be quite helpful.

Do not be misled, however, by surface appearances. Remember that the exposure to the same conditions and facts may be interpreted entirely differently by another person. For this reason, do not depend completely on personal observations or personal experiences for information. Every statement given as fact in a research paper must unquestionably be based on validated information.

Personal Interviews

Interviewing persons who are knowledgeable about a topic lends human interest to the research project. Talking with such people may also prevent chasing up blind alleys and may supply information unobtainable elsewhere.

Since methods of getting facts in interviews require almost as much thought as the methods involved in library work, interviewing should be carried out systematically. The first thing to remember is courtesy. In seeking an appointment for an interview, request cooperation tactfully. Secondly, give thoughtful preparation to the interview. Be businesslike in manner and prepare your questions in advance. Finally, keep careful notes of the interview. In quoting the person interviewed, be sure to use his exact words and his intended meaning. And remember, although the personal interview is a valuable source of information, it offers only one person's opinions.

Free and Inexpensive Materials from Various Agencies

Many agencies distribute free or inexpensive pamphlets, documents, and reports that contain much valuable information. The

U. S. Government Printing Office, the various departments of the United States government, industries, insurance companies, labor unions, and professional organizations are just a few of the sources that may supply excellent material on a subject.

In seeking material from various agencies, be sure that the request is *specific*. For instance, a student writing a library paper on state requirements for teaching high school English might be disappointed in the response to his request to state departments of education for "information on teaching English." Such a request is difficult, if not impossible, to fill because the *particular* need is not specified. A request for "information concerning requirements in your state for teaching high school English," however, specifies the subject and thus encourages a more satisfactory response.

In writing for materials, there is, of course, the time element involved. Do not assume that all or even most of the information for your paper will come from these requested materials. Depending too much on what you *hope* to receive before the deadline date for the paper could be disastrous.

Library Materials

Most of the information for a research paper is in the library. Printed materials, particularly books and periodicals, will provide most of the needed data. Audiovisual materials may also be helpful.

The library contains a world of information, but that information is of little value unless you know how to find it. Fortunately for the researcher, much of the work in locating information on a subject has already been done. You do not have to look through every book and every issue of every periodical in the library to see if they contain information on your subject. The information in books and magazines has been cataloged and indexed so that finding it is quite simple. Once you are familiar with the card catalog, the library's system of classifying books, the indexes to periodicals, and the periodical holdings list, you are well on your way toward finding whatever information you need.

THE CARD CATALOG

The card catalog is a series of file drawers containing at least one 3-by-5-inch card for each publication in the library. The cards are filed alphabetically according to the first important word in the heading (first line) on the card.

Nonfiction books—the books most often used for a library paper—have at least three cards for each book: author card, title card, and subject card. Only the heading of each card is different; the other information is the same. Here is an example of a subject card; encircled numbers have been added to correspond to the explanatory notes that follow.

---

①
301.47   ②
C18c   The college drug scene.

③-Carey, James T   ⑤
④-The college drug scene [by] James T. Carey. Englewood
Cliffs, N.J., Prentice-Hall [1968]-⑦
          ⑨   ⑥   ⑩
⑧-ix, 210 p. 21 cm. (A Spectrum book) $5.95-⑫
⑬-Bibliographical footnotes.   ⑪

          ⑭   ⑮
     1. Narcotics and youth—Berkeley, Calif. 2. Narcotic habit—
Berkeley, Calif.   I. Title.-⑯
⑰-HV5831.C2C36   ⑲-68—27489
               ⑱-301.47'686'30979467
⑳-Library of Congress   ㉑-[69p7]

Subject Card

1. Call number. This is the designation used for classifying and shelving the book.

2. Heading. This is a subject card; therefore the subject, usually typed in red, is on the first line.

3. Author's name, usually followed by year of birth and year of death.

4. Complete title of book.

5. City of publication.

6. Publishing company.

7. Date of publication.

8. Number of pages of introductory material.

9. Number of pages in the book.

10.   Height in centimeters.

11.   Publisher's series.

12.   Cost.

13.   Notation of a special feature.

14., 15., 16.   Other ways in which the book is cataloged.

17.   Library of Congress Classification number.

18.   Dewey Decimal Classification number.

19.   Library of Congress catalog card number.

20.   Indication that this card was printed at the Library of Congress.

21.   Qualities of the card itself.

As you begin looking in the card catalog for books containing information on your subject, you may not know any authors or titles to consult. If so, consult the subject cards. Suppose you were writing a paper on "Medical Applications of the Laser." If you do not know any titles or authors concerning the subject, look first in the "L" file drawer for "Laser." However, do not stop after looking under the one subject heading, "Laser"; look under other related subject headings. Some of the most important information might be cataloged under such subjects as "Medicine," "Surgery," or "Physics."

SYSTEMS OF CLASSIFYING BOOKS

Libraries classify books according to one of two systems: the Library of Congress Classification or the Dewey Decimal Classification. The Library of Congress Classification uses letters of the alphabet to divide all books into twenty basic groups. These basic groups have many divisions, designated by a letter-number combination. The main classes are:

A   General works

B   Philosophy, psychology, religion

C   History, auxiliary sciences

D   History and topography (except America)

E and F   American history

G   Geography, anthropology

H   Social sciences

J   Political science

K   Law

L   Education

M	Music	S	Agriculture, plant and animal industry
N	Fine arts		
P	Languages and literature	T	Technology
		U	Military science
Q	Science	V	Naval science
R	Medicine	Z	Bibliography, library science

The more common system, the one that most libraries follow, is the Dewey Decimal Classification, which uses numbers to divide all books into ten basic groups:

000	General works	500	Pure sciences
100	Philosophy and related disciplines	600	Technology (Applied sciences)
200	Religion	700	The arts
300	Social sciences	800	Literature
400	Language	900	History, geography, biography

These basic groups are divided and then subdivided numerous times.

As an example of the differences in the two classifying systems, the book *The Pyrenees*, by Hilaire Belloc, has the following designations:

Library of Congress	Dewey Decimal
DP302.P8B4	914.6

ESSAY INDEX

It is often difficult to locate essays and miscellaneous articles in books. *The Essay and General Literature Index* is an index by author, subject, and some titles, of essays and articles published in books since 1900. The index is kept up to date by supplements.

INDEXES TO PERIODICALS

Periodical indexes are to periodicals what the card catalog is to books. By consulting indexes to periodicals, specific sources of information on a subject can be found without having to look through hundreds of thousands of magazines.

In writing a library paper, two indexes in particular will be useful: the *Readers' Guide to Periodical Literature* (generally referred to as the *Readers' Guide*) and the *Social Sciences and Hu-*

manities Index. At the beginning of all periodical indexes, there are directions for use, a key to abbreviations, and a list of magazines indexed.

The *Readers' Guide* is a general index of over a hundred and fifty leading popular magazines published from 1900 to the present. There are two issues a month, except for July and August, when there is only one issue a month. The second issue of each month includes the material from the first issue of the month. There are other cumulative issues every three months, every year, and every two years. This cumulation saves you from having to look in many different issues and keeps the index up to date.

Articles in the *Readers' Guide* are indexed under author, subject, and title (if necessary). Each entry gives the title of the article, the author (if known), the name of the magazine, the volume, the page numbers, and additional notations for such items as bibliography, illustrations, or portrait. The excerpt below, from an issue of the *Readers' Guide,**** is the complete listing of all "Wildlife" entries.

WILDLIFE
Vanishing wildlife. il Time 95: 52+ Je 8 '70
Wildlife of Sinai. W. Ferguson. il Audubon 72:32-41 Mr '70
WILDLIFE conservation
Mike Frome; endangered tule elk. M. Frome. Am For 76:3+ My '70
See also
Bird sanctuaries
National wildlife federation
Laws and legislation
Survival of species; Endangered species conservation act. A. W. Smith. Nat Parks & Con Mag 44:2 Je '70
Australia
Kangaroos, states and conservation. W. Scholes. Sci N 97:564 Je 6 '70
California
Bighorns: wild sheep of California. L. L. Lutz. il Am For 76:28-31 My; 30-1+ Je '70

Idaho
Showdown on the Salmon River range; attempt to save Idaho's bighorns. R. Woodbury. il pors Life 68:54-56A My 22 '70
South Dakota
Reporter at large; controlling the prairie dog and protecting the black-footed ferret. F. McNulty. New Yorker 46:40-2+ Je 13 '70
WILDLIFE control. See Animal populations—Control
WILDLIFE photography. See Photography of animals
WILDLIFE sanctuaries
See also
Bird sanctuaries
New York (state)
Sanctuary on the subway; Jamaica Bay wildlife refuge. F. Graham, jr. il Audubon 72: 54-9 My '70

---

*Reprinted by permission of the H. W. Wilson Company.

The first entry in the listing indicates that there is an illustrated article entitled "Vanishing Wildlife" in *Time*, Volume 95, page 52 and continued on other pages in the June 8, 1970, issue. Note that in the "Wildlife conservation" entry there are *See also* cross-references to related subject areas.

Published since 1916, the *Social Sciences and Humanities Index* (until 1965 the *International Index*) indexes some two hundred scholarly journals in the humanities and social sciences. Current numbers are issued quarterly. Cumulative numbers are issued for one, two, three, and four years. Articles are indexed under author and subject in the same way that they are in the *Readers' Guide*.

The primary difference between the *Social Sciences and Humanities Index* and the *Readers' Guide* is the type of periodicals indexed in each: The *Social Sciences and Humanities Index* covers more scholarly periodicals, and the *Readers' Guide* indexes periodicals of a broad, general, and popular character.

In addition to the *Reader's Guide* and the *Social Sciences and Humanities Index*, there are other general indexes as well as numerous indexes in specific fields, such as *Applied Arts Index, Biological and Agricultural Index, Business Periodicals Index, Cumulative Index to Nursing Literature, Engineering Index,* and *MLA International Bibliography of Books and Articles on the Modern Languages and Literature.*

PERIODICALS HOLDING LIST

The periodicals holdings list is a catalog of all the periodicals in a library. This list gives the name of each magazine and the dates of the available issues. The list may also indicate whether the issues are bound or unbound and where in the library the magazines are located.

The periodicals holdings list may be in various forms, such as a drawer of 3-by-5-inch cards, a visible index file, a typed sheet, or an automated printout. Some libraries combine the periodicals holdings list with the card catalog.

It is essential to know where the periodicals holdings list in a library is located. When titles of articles that seem promising are found in the various periodical indexes, you must know if the library has the specified magazines. The periodicals holdings list will tell you. Remember, however, that if the school library does not have a magazine, other libraries in the area may. Investigate public libraries, libraries in other schools, the libraries of businesses and industries, and personal libraries of classmates and friends.

VERTICAL FILE

Much printed information exists in other than book and magazine forms. Pamphlets, booklets, bulletins, clippings, and other miscellaneous unbound materials are usually in a collection called the veritical file. These materials are filed or cataloged by subject. The vertical file and the *Vertical File Index*, which lists current pamphlets, are valuable sources of information.

REFERENCE WORKS

Numerous guides are available for using reference books. Most guides explain the arrangement of libraries and of their materials. They discuss in detail general periodical indexes, dictionaries, encyclopedias, and yearbooks. The guide books also give basic reference works in specific subject areas, such as science and technology, literature, music, religion, the social sciences, and biography. Ask your librarian to suggest an up-to-date guide for your use.

Often, a good starting point for locating information about your subject and for gaining an overall view of it is a general reference book. Listed below are some of the more useful general reference works. (For a list of dictionaries, see page 125.)

1.   General encyclopedias (each is kept up to date with an annual supplement)

> *Collier's Encyclopedia* (24 vols.)
> *Compton's Pictured Encyclopedia* (18 vols.)
> *Encyclopedia Americana* (30 vols.)
> *Encyclopaedia Britannica* (24 vols.)
> *Encyclopedia International* (20 vols.)
> *World Book Encyclopedia* (20 vols.)

2.   Yearbooks and books of facts

> *Facts on File: World News Digest* (since 1940)
> *Information Please Almanac* (since 1947)
> *International Yearbook and Statesmen's Who's Who* (since 1953)

> *Statesman's Year-book: Statistical and Historical Annual of the States of the World* (since 1864)
> *Statistical Abstract of the United States* (since 1879)
> *World Almanac and Book of Facts* (since 1868)
> *United Nations Statistical Year Book* (since 1948)

3. General biographical reference works

> *Biography Index* (since 1946)
> *Chamber's Biographical Dictionary: The Great of All Nations and All Times* (rev. ed. 1962)
> *Current Biography: Who's News and Why* (since 1940)
> *Dictionary of American Biography* (11 vols.)
> *Dictionary of National Biography* (22 vols. and supplements)
> *International Who's Who* (since 1935)
> *Webster's Biographical Dictionary* (1964)
> *Who's Who* (since 1849)
> *Who's Who in America* (since 1899)

AUDIOVISUAL MATERIALS

Most colleges have an audiovisual department, a media center, or a library department that supervises audiovisual materials. Check with the librarian or person in charge concerning the cataloging of such materials as audio tapes, video tapes, phonograph recordings, films, filmstrips, and slides. They may contain valuable information on your subject.

Through the advances in microphotography, reading material is increasingly being stored in the space-saving forms of microfilm, microfiche, and ultramicrofiche. In these methods the printed material is recorded on film. When a person wants to read the film, he puts it into a machine that magnifies it. Check the microfilm, microfiche, and ultramicrofiche holdings in the library for possible helpful material. A librarian can explain how and where these materials are cataloged.

Compiling a Working Bibliography

Familiar now with the four general sources of information—personal observation or experience, personal interviews, free and inexpensive material from various agencies, and library materials—

you are ready to list possible specific sources of information for your research paper. This list is called the *working bibliography*. Record each possible source on a separate bibliography card. To save time later, record the information in the same order and form in which it will be presented in the final bibliography. Do not follow the form used in an index such as the *Readers' Guide to Periodical Literature;* such a space-saving system is not generally used except by the index.

Most of the possible sources of information for the paper will be books, magazines, and pamphlets (*pamphlet* is used here to include reports, brochures, bulletins, etc.) On the following pages, therefore, are directions for recording bibliographical data for a book, a section of a book, a magazine article, an encyclopedia article, and a pamphlet. Forms for other bibliographical sources are given on pages 209–212.

BIBLIOGRAPHY CARD FOR A BOOK

For each book that is a possible source of information, write the following data on a card:

1.   Author's or editor's full name (last name first).

2.   Title of the book (underlined).

3.   Edition (if other than the first).

4.   Volume number (if the work is in several volumes).

5.   City of publication.

6.   Publishing company.

7.   Date of publication.

8.   Call number. (Including the call number of the book saves time by making it unnecessary to go back to the card catalog when ready to use the book. The lower or upper left-hand corner of the card is a good place for the call number.)

In addition, it may be helpful to write the following information on the bibliography card:

9.   Notation as to the nature or contents of the book.

10.   Library in which the book is located. (This is a time-saver if several libraries are used. Place the name of the library, or an abbreviation for it, in the lower or upper left-hand corner, below the call number.)

Example: Bibliography Card for a Book

Higham, Charles

The Films of Orson Welles.
Berkeley: University of
California Press, 1970.
    Illustrations

Personal Library

BIBLIOGRAPHY CARD FOR A SECTION OF A BOOK

If a possible source of information is a section, chapter, or essay in a book, record the following data on a bibliography card:

1.   Author of the section (last name first).

2.   Title of the section (in quotation marks).

3.   Title of the book (underlined).

4.   Author or editor of the book, if different from the author of the section.

5.   City of publication.

6. Publishing company.

7. Date of publication.

8. Page numbers of the section.

Example: Bibliography Card for a Section of a Book

```
Untermeyer, Louis
 "Isadora Duncan", Makers of the
modern World. New York: Simon
and Schuster, 1955, pp. 522-532.


    920
    Un 8m
    College Library
```

BIBLIOGRAPHY CARD FOR A MAGAZINE ARTICLE

On each bibliography card for a magazine article, record:

1. Author's name (last name first), if given.

2. Title of the article (in quotation marks).

3. Title of the magazine (underlined).

4. Volume number.

5. Date of publication (in parentheses).

6. Page numbers.

Example: Bibliography Card for a Magazine Article

Spackman, Bob

"a new approach to strength Building". *athletic journal*,
51 (Jan., 1971), 39, 69-71.

796.05
A871
College Library

BIBLIOGRAPHY CARD FOR AN ENCYCLOPEDIA ARTICLE

For a bibliography card for an encyclopedia article, record:

1.   Author's name (last name first), if given. Encyclopedia articles are often signed with initials; it may be necessary to look in a separate listing for identification of the initials.

2.   Title of the article (in quotation marks).

3.   Name of the encyclopedia (underlined). If the source is an annual supplement, so indicate with the appropriate term: Annual, Yearbook, etc.

4.   Year of publication.

Volume and page numbers are unnecessary for articles in alphabetically arranged references.

Example: Bibliography Card for an Encyclopedia Article

Leicester, Henry M.

"Alchemy", Encyclopedia
Americana, 1971.

AE
5
E333
1970
University Library

BIBLIOGRAPHY CARD FOR A PAMPHLET

For a bibliography card for a pamphlet or for any individual, printed work of less than book length, give the following:

1. Author's or editor's name, if given (last name first), or if an organization is considered the author, its name.

2. Title of the pamphlet (underlined).

3. Other identifying information, such as series name and number.

4. City of publication.

5. Publishing company.

6. Date of publication.

Example: Bibliography Card for a Pamphlet

> Copyright Office, the Library
> of Congress
>
> Copyright Law of the United
> States of America, Bulletin No. 14.
> Washington, D.C. : U.S. Government
> Printing Office, 1967.

STEP III. RECORDING AND ORGANIZING THE FACTS

A key step in writing a successful library paper is recording and organizing information. This step involves evaluating resource material, taking notes, stating the central idea of a paper, constructing a formal outline, and arranging the note cards to fit the outline.

Evaluating Resource Material

You must *evaluate* resource material; all sources are not equally useful or reliable. It is important to know the difference between primary and secondary sources, to separate fact from opinion, and to use nontextual qualities of a source in evaluating it.

Primary sources are firsthand accounts of an event or condition. In a paper on the development of Salk polio vaccine, for instance, material by Dr. Salk would be a primary source. Secondary sources are works written about firsthand accounts. A magazine article about

Dr. Salk would be a secondary source. Although secondary sources are generally more readily available, use primary sources whenever possible.

Separating fact from opinion is essential in evaluating a source. A fact is an item of information that can be proved, such as, "The book has 450 pages" or "*Tender Is the Night* is a novel by F. Scott Fitzgerald." An opinion is an interpretation of a fact, or an idea about a fact, such as, "This book has 450 *exciting* pages" or "*Tender Is the Night* is F. Scott Fitzgerald's *best* novel." You must be able to distinguish facts from opinions.

The nontextual qualities of a source may be helpful in evaluation. The reputation of the author and of the publishing company, date of publication, table of contents, introductory material, bibliography, index—each gives an indication of the usefulness and reliability of a source. For instance, an article about the surface of the moon written in 1968 would not be as reliable as an article written by Armstrong and Aldrin after their moon landing in 1969.

Taking Notes

In investigating each source in the working bibliography, save time by first consulting the table of contents and the index for the exact pages that may contain helpful information. After locating the information, scan it to get the general idea. Then, if the information is of value, read it carefully. If certain material may be specifically used in the paper, write it down on note cards.

DIRECT QUOTATIONS

Some notes will be direct quotations, that is, the author's exact words. There may be passages in which the author has been particularly concise and skillful in his wording, and thus his exact words are written on the note card. Generally, take few note cards as direct quotations because they create a greater tendency to rely on someone else's phrasing and organization for the paper. If it is desirable to leave out a part of a quotation, use an ellipsis mark, that is, three spaced periods (. . .) or four spaced periods if the omission includes an end period. Be sure to put quotation marks around all quoted material.

Note Card—Direct Quotation

sensation of time on the moon

armstrong
p. 2

" There was a peculiar sensation of the duality of time - the swift rush of events that characterizes all our lives - and the ponderous parade which makes the aging of the universe. Both kinds of time were evident - the first by the routine events of the flight ... the latter by rocks around us, unchanged throughout the history of man."

PARAPHRASES AND SUMMARIES

Most of the notes for a library paper will be paraphrases and summaries rather than direct quotations. A paraphrase is a restatement in different words of someone else's statement. A summary is the gist, or main points, of a passage or article. In reading, get main ideas and record them in your own words. Jot down key phrases and sentences that summarize ideas clearly. Do not bother taking down isolated details and useless illustrative material. It is not necessary to write notes in complete sentences, but each note should be sensible, factual, and legible—and meaningful to you after two weeks.

General Directions for Taking Notes

Regardless of the shortcuts you have devised for taking notes, following these directions will be the shortest shortcut:

1. Take notes in ink on either 3-by-5 or 4-by-6-inch cards. Ink is more legible than pencil, and cards are easier to handle than pieces of paper.

Note Card—Paraphrase

diesel economy   Jones
                                  p. 41

In big tractors about two
gallons of diesel fuel do the
work of three gallons of gasoline.

Note Card—Summary

characteristics   Davis
                             pp. 46-47
Indoor/outdoor carpets:
   must consist entirely of man-made
   fibers that are moisture resistant
Won't rot or mildew
Don't shrink
Not harmed by summer heat or
   winter cold
Don't fade
Can be kept clean by vacuuming
   or by hosing with water

2. If it is difficult to decide when to take notes and when not to, quit *trying* to take notes. Read a half dozen or so of the sources, taking no notes. Study the preliminary outline (do not hesitate to revise the outline—it is purely for your use). Then return to the sources with a clearer idea of what facts you really need.

3. Write only one item of information on each note card.

4. Always write notes from different sources on different cards.

5. Take brief notes—passages that may possibly be quoted in the paper, statistics, and other such specific data, proper names, dates, and only enough other information to jog the memory. Writing naturally or well cannot be done if the paper is based solely on notes rather than your overall knowledge and understanding.

6. Write a key word or phrase indicating the content of each note card in the upper left corner for quick reference and for classification according to topic.

7. In the upper right corner, identify the source (author's name and, if necessary, title of the work) and give the specific page number from which the information comes.

8. Remember that proper credit must be given in the paper for all borrowed material—quotations, exact figures, or information and ideas that are not widely known among educated people. Remember, too, that an idea stated in your own words is just as much borrowed as an idea quoted in the author's exact words.

Stating the Central Idea and Constructing a Formal Outline

At the very beginning of the research project you formulated a basic question or problem to be answered; then you divided this general question into specific questions, or aspects, as a preliminary outline. As investigation progressed, you added to, changed, and perhaps even omitted some of the original questions. Thus, your present list of questions looks quite different from the beginning list. (If the preliminary outline has not been brought up to date, it should be revised after you have taken all your notes.)

By this stage in the research you should have clearly in mind the central idea of your paper. Write this central idea (thesis statement or controlling idea) as a one-sentence summary at the top of what will be the working-outline page. (For further treatment of central idea see pages 98–99.)

From the central idea, the list of questions or divisions in the revised preliminary outline, and the key words in the upper left corner of the note cards, structure a formal outline to serve as the working outline for the first draft of the paper. Every major division in the outline should reflect a major aspect of the central idea. All of the major divisions, taken as a whole, should cover the central idea and adequately explain it.

The formal outline may be either a sentence outline or a topic outline. In a sentence outline all the headings are complete statements (no heading should be a question), and in a topic outline all the headings are phrases or single words. The sentence outline is more complete and helps to clarify your thinking on each point as you go along; it brings you one step nearer the writing of the paper. The topic outline is briefer and shows at a glance the divisions and subdivisions of the subject. Whichever type of outline you choose, be consistent; do not mix topics and sentences. (For further treatment of outlining, see pages 98–99).

The working outline serves as a work plan in writing the first draft of the paper; it lets you know where you are and provides a systematic organization of the information.

Arranging the Note Cards to Fit the Outline

When the working outline is completed, mark each note card with a Roman numeral, letter of the alphabet, or Arabic numeral to show to what section and subsection of the outline the note card corresponds. Then rearrange the note cards accordingly. If the note cards are insufficient, look up additional material; if there are irrelevant note cards, discard them. When there seems to be just the right amount of material to cover each point in the outline adequately, you are ready to begin writing the paper. Each main heading in the outline should correspond to a major section of the paper; each subheading to a supporting section. In a well-developed paper the main idea in every paragraph will correspond to a heading in the outline.

STEP IV.   REPORTING THE FACTS

The First Draft

With the working outline for a guide and the note cards for content, write rapidly and freely the first draft of the paper. Concentrate on getting thoughts down on paper in logical order; take care of grammar, punctuation, and mechanical points later. In writing the first draft, it will be necessary to write short transitional passages to connect the material on the note cards. Also, it will be necessary to rephrase notes (except for direct quotations) to suit the exact thought and style of writing.

Introduction and Conclusion

In the first paragraph, or in a section entitled "Introduction," restate the thesis, or central idea, of the paper. Let the reader know what he is to expect. Let him know to what extent the subject will be explored, as indicated in the major headings of the outline. After completing the body of the paper, close with a paragraph that is a summary, a climax, or a conclusion drawn from the material you have presented.

Quotations and Paraphrases

If the exact words of another writer are used, put them in quotation marks. If the quotation is in verse or is an extended prose passage, however, instead of using quotation marks, indent from both the left and right margins each line of the quoted matter. This indented material is called an *extract*.

Incorporate paraphrased matter and indirect quotations into the body of the paper, and do not use quotation marks. In footnotes acknowledge *all* borrowed information, whether presented in another writer's words or paraphrased.

Footnotes

In general, footnotes serve three specific purposes: to give authority for statements presented, to acknowledge borrowed material, and to give additional information. Whatever the purpose of a footnote, however, certain conventions of spacing, numbering, and form should be observed.

SPACING AND NUMBERING OF FOOTNOTES

1.   Place footnotes on a separate sheet at the end of the composition rather than at the bottom of the respective pages, unless instructed otherwise.

2.   Indicate footnotes with a superscript number (a number slightly above the regular line of type) following the term or statement of reference. There is no space between the superscript and the preceding word. No punctuation is used after the superscript in either the body or the footnote.

3.   Number footnotes consecutively throughout the paper. If, for instance, there are two footnotes on page one and one footnote on page two, the footnote on page two would be number three.

4.   Double space between separate footnotes and between the lines of one footnote. Indent the first line of each footnote as if it were a paragraph.

FORMS OF FOOTNOTES

1.   For each source referred to in the text of the paper, give in a footnote the necessary bibliographical information: author, work, publishing data, date, and page numbers.

2.   If reference is made to a source for which bibliographical information has already been given in a footnote, do not repeat the information; use a shortened footnote form.

3.   Ibid. (abbreviation for the Latin *ibidem*, "the same") is the shortened form to use if the source is the same as that in the immediately preceding footnote or if only the page number is different from that in the immediately preceding footnote. Since ibid. is an abbreviation, it should be followed by a period.

4.   If reference is made to a source in an earlier, but not immediately preceding footnote, give only the author's last name and the page number. (Remember that ibid. refers only to the immediately preceding source.)

EXAMPLES OF FOOTNOTES

The following examples of footnotes illustrate various aspects of mechanics and form. Listed on pages 209–213 and page 214 are other examples of footnotes.

[1]Howard T. Walden, *Familiar Fresh Water Fishes of America* (New York: Harper, 1964), p. 81.

[2]Ibid., p. 173.

[3]O. A. Battista, ed., *Synthetic Fibers in Papermaking* (New York: Wiley, 1964), p. 94.

[4]Walden, p. 83.

Revising the Outline and the First Draft

After writing the first draft of the paper, study it carefully for accuracy of content, mechanical correctness, logical organization, clarity, proportion, and general effectiveness. Check to see if the intended reader has been kept in mind. You may understand perfectly well what you have written, but the real test of writing skill is whether or not the reader will understand the paper.

Make needed revisions in the outline and the first draft. This may mean making several drafts of the outline and paper. But, after the hours, days, and weeks already invested in this project, a few more hours polishing the paper is worth the effort. Careful revision may mean the difference between an A and a D paper.

Bibliography

From the working bibliography make an alphabetical list of all the books, articles, and other materials that were actually used in writing the paper. Besides the sources referred to in footnotes, list all the references from which you gained a general knowledge of the subject. Listed on pages 209–213 are examples of bibliographical forms.

Give a precise, appropriate label to the bibliography page, such as "List of Works Consulted," "List of Works Cited," "A Selected Bibliography," or "A Brief Annotated Bibliography."

The Final Paper

When the outline, the text of the paper, the footnotes, and the bibliography are completed, carefully recopy them. Follow the general format directions for theme writing and remember to double space the entire paper. In a handwritten paper, space it as if it were typewritten.

Proofread the paper thoroughly. Clip the pages together in this order: title page, outline (if required), body of the paper, footnotes (or notes), and bibliography.

BIBLIOGRAPHICAL AND FOOTNOTE FORMS

The following pages suggest bibliographical and footnote forms for the kinds of sources you are most likely to use in writing a library paper. For each kind of entry indicated on the left, there is first a bibliographical entry and second a footnote entry for the same source. These suggested forms follow *The MLA Style Sheet*, 2nd ed. New York: Modern Language Association, 1970. (Note that the material appearing here in italic type would be underlined in a typewritten or handwritten paper.)

I. Books

One author

Stromberg, Ann. *Philanthropic Foundations in Latin America*. New York: Russell Sage Foundation, 1968.

[1]Ann Stromberg, *Philanthropic Foundations in Latin America* (New York: Russell Sage Foundation, 1968), p. 81.

Two or three authors

Durelli, A. J., and W. F. Riley. *Introduction to Photomechanics*. Englewood Cliffs, N.J.: Prentice-Hall, 1965.

[2]A. J. Durelli and W. F. Riley, *Introduction to Photomechanics* (Englewood Cliffs, N.J.: Prentice-Hall, 1965), p. 131.

More than three authors

Jensen, Jorgen, et al. *Design Guide to Orbital Flight*. New York: McGraw-Hill, 1962.

[3]Jorgen Jensen et al., *Design Guide to Orbital Flight* (New York: McGraw-Hill, 1962), p. 12.

Editor

Battista, O. A., ed. *Synthetic Fibers in Papermaking*. New York: Wiley, 1964.

[4]O. A. Battista, ed., *Synthetic Fibers in Papermaking* (New York: Wiley, 1964), pp. 107–108.

Editor, text by another	Crane, Hart. *The Collected Poems of Hart Crane*, ed. Waldo Frank. New York: Liveright, 1933. ⁵Hart Crane, *The Collected Poems of Hart Crane*, ed. Waldo Frank (New York: Liveright, 1933), p. 17.
Several vols., separate titles	Purcell, E. M. *Electricity and Magnetism*, Vol. II of *Berkeley Physics Course*. New York: McGraw-Hill, 1965. ⁶E. M. Purcell, *Electricity and Magnetism*, Vol. II of *Berkeley Physics Course* (New York: McGraw-Hill, 1965), p. 129.
Book in series	Fry, Thornton C. *Probability and Its Engineering Uses*, 2nd ed. Bell Telephone Labortories Series. Princeton, N. J.: Van Nostrand, 1965. ⁷Thornton C. Fry, *Probability and Its Engineering Uses*, 2nd ed., Bell Telephone Laboratories Series (Princeton, N. J.: Van Nostrand, 1965), p. 57.
Modern reprint	Dunne, Finley Peter. *Mr. Dooley in Peace and in War*. 1898; rpt. St. Clair Shores, Mich.: Scholarly Press, 1968. ⁸Finley Peter Dunne, *Mr. Dooley in Peace and in War* (1898; rpt. St. Clair Shores, Mich.: Scholarly Press, 1968), p. 93.

II.   Encyclopedia Articles

Article signed with initials	T[illyard], E. M. W. "John Milton," *Chambers Encyclopaedia*, 1966. ⁹E. M. W. T[illyard], "John Milton," *Chambers Encyclopaedia* (1966).
Unsigned article	"Yam," *Encyclopaedia Britannica*, 1971. ¹⁰"Yam," *Encyclopaedia Britannica* (1971).

III.   Essays or Sections of Books

Essay from "casebook"	Savage, S. S. "The Significance of F. Scott Fitzgerald." *Arizona Quarterly*, 8 (Autumn 1952). Rpt. in Arthur Mizener, ed. *F. Scott Fitzgerald: A Col-*

lection of Critical Essays, Twentieth Century
Views. Englewood Cliffs, N. J.: Prentice-Hall,
1963, pp. 146–156.
    ¹¹D. S. Savage, "The Significance of F. Scott Fitz-
gerald," *Arizona Quarterly,* 8 (Autumn 1952), rpt. in
Arthur Mizener, ed., *F. Scott Fitzgerald: A Collection of Critical Essays,* Twentieth Century Views
(Englewood Cliffs, N. J.: Prentice-Hall, 1963), p. 155.

Essay	Untermeyer, Louis. "Auguste Rodin," *Makers of the Modern World.* New York: Simon & Schuster, 1955, pp. 170–176. ¹²Louis Untermeyer, "Auguste Rodin," *Makers of the Modern World* (New York: Simon & Schuster, 1955), p. 174.
Essay in an anthology	Levinson, Harry. "Alcoholism in Industry," *Health and the Community,* ed. Alfred H. Katz and Jean Spencer Felton. New York: Free Press, 1965, pp. 187–191. ¹³Harry Levinson, "Alcoholism in Industry," *Health and the Community,* ed. Alfred H. Katz and Jean Spencer Felton (New York: Free Press, 1965), p. 187.

IV. Periodicals

Unsigned newspaper article	"Antitank System Designed by Bonn," *New York Times,* 16 Aug. 1970, p. 3, col. 6. ¹⁴"Antitank System Designed by Bonn," *New York Times,* 16 Aug. 1970, p. 3, col. 6.
Signed newspaper article; city inserted for clarity	Rand, Clayton."Increase in Drugs Eyed." [New Orleans] *Times-Picayune,* 22 Aug. 1970, p. 8, cols. 4–5. ¹⁵Clayton Rand, "Increase in Drugs Eyed," [New Orleans] *Times-Picayune,* 22 Aug. 1970, p. 8, col. 4.
Signed magazine article	Pizer, Donald. "Frank Norris' Definition of Naturalism." *Modern Fiction Studies,* 8 (Winter 1963), 408–410.

[16]Donald Pizer, "Frank Norris' Definition of Naturalism," *Modern Fiction Studies*, 8 (Winter 1963), 409.

Unsigned "Change and Turmoil on Wall Street." *Time*, 24 Aug.
magazine 1970, pp. 52–57.
article [17]"Change and Turmoil on Wall Street," *Time*, 24 Aug. 1970, p. 52.

V. Publications, Miscellaneous

Pamphlet American Chemical Society. *Plasticization and*
by an *Plasticizer Processes*, Advances in Chemistry
organization Series. No. 48. Washington, D. C.: The Society, 1965.
[18]American Chemical Society, *Plasticization and Plasticizer Processes*, Advances in Chemistry Series, No. 48 (Washington, D. C.: The Society, 1965), p. 9.

Signed Willner, Ann Ruth. *Charismatic Political Leader-*
report *ship; A Theory*, Research Monograph No. 32. Princeton, N.J.: Center of International Studies, Princeton Univ., 1968.
[19]Ann Ruth Willner, *Charismatic Political Leadership; A Theory*, Research Monograph No. 32 (Princeton, N. J.: Center of International Studies, Princeton Univ., 1968), p. 37.

VI. Nonprinted Materials

Interview James, Clyde D., Personnel Manager, Quality Manu-
(or lecture facturing Company. Personal interview on desir-
or speech) able characteristics in new employees. St. Louis, Missouri, 10 Nov. 1971.
[20]Clyde D. James, Personnel Manager, Quality Manufacturing Company. Personal Interview on desirable characteristics in new employees. St. Louis, Missouri, 10 Nov. 1971.

Television *(or radio)* *program*	"Camera Three," WJTV television, 6 July 1969. "A Modern Day Forger, Part 2." Host, James Macandrew. [21]"Camera Three," WJTV television, 6 July 1969. "A Modern Day Forger, Part 2." Host, James Macandrew.
Audio *(or video* *tape)*	*Frank Lloyd Wright—Architect of Vision.* Audio Tape. New York Board of Education, 1966. [22]*Frank Lloyd Wright—Architect of Vision*, audio tape, New York Board of Education, 1966.
Film *(or* *filmstrip)*	*Time Lapse Photography.* Film. Chicago: International Film Bureau, 1961. [23]*Time Lapse Photography*, film, International Film Bureau, 1961.

EXCERPTS FROM A LIBRARY PAPER

The following excerpts from a student's library paper, "Hemingway's Santiago as Tragic Hero," illustrate the basics of documentation. The two paragraphs indicate the kind of material that is footnoted. The Footnotes and the Selected Bibliography illustrate standard footnote and bibliographical forms.

Hemingway's Santiago as Tragic Hero

. . . .

As Clinton S. Burhams, Jr., points out, *The Old Man and the Sea* is the culminating expression of Hemingway's mature view of the tragic irony of man's fate.[4] This tragic irony is epitomized in the heroic individualism of the old fisherman, Santiago, and his struggle with the great fish and his relentless fight against the sharks. Santiago, after the first attack from the sharks, realizes his predicament:

It was too good to last, he thought, I wish it had been a dream now and that I had never hooked the fish and was alone in bed on the newspapers.

"But man is not made for defeat," he said. "A man can be destroyed but not defeated," I am sorry that I killed the fish though, he thought.[5]

. . . .

But in Santiago's cosmic struggle, that which would destroy (the sharks) is the literal winner. He declares to the big fish, " 'I am sorry that I went too far out. I ruined us both' " (p. 127). The old man's victory is the "moral victory of having lasted without permanent impairment of his belief in the worth of what he has been doing."[9]

Footnotes

[1]Philip Young, *Ernest Hemingway*, Univ. of Minnesota Pamphlets on American Writers, No. 1 (Minneapolis: Univ. of Minn. Press, 1959), p. 17.

[2]Melvin Backman, "Hemingway: The Matador and the Crucified," *Hemingway and His Critics: An International Anthology*, ed. Carlos Baker (New York: Hill and Wang, 1961), p. 250.

[3]Ibid., p. 257.

[4]*"The Old Man and the Sea*: Hemingway's Tragic Vision of Man," *American Literature*, 31 (Jan. 1960), 447.

[5]Ernest Hemingway, *The Old Man and the Sea* (New York: Scribner's, 1952), p. 114. All references to the novel are from this edition. Subsequent page references are given in parentheses in the text, following each quotation or citation.

[6]Sheridan Baker, *Ernest Hemingway: An Introduction and Interpretation* (New York: Barnes and Noble, 1967), p. 68.

[7]Backman, p. 246.

[8]Sheridan Baker, p. 140.

[9]Carlos Baker, *Hemingway: The Writer as Artist* (Princeton, N. J.: Princeton Univ. Press, 1956), p. 295.

[10]Ibid.

[11]Philip Young, *Ernest Hemingway* (New York: Rinehart, 1952), p. 106.

[12]Philip Young, *Ernest Hemingway*, Univ. of Minnesota Pamphlets on American Writers, p. 12.

Selected Bibliography

Backman, Melvin. "Hemingway: The Matador and the Crucified," *Hemingway and His Critics; An International Anthology*, ed. Carlos Baker. New York: Hill and Wang, 1961, pp. 245–258.

Baker, Carlos. *Hemingway: The Writer as Artist*. Princeton, N.J.: Princeton Univ. Press, 1956.

Baker, Sheridan. *Ernest Hemingway: An Introduction and Interpretation.* New York: Barnes and Noble, 1967.

Burhans, Clinton S., Jr. *"The Old Man and the Sea*: Hemingway's Tragic Vision of Man." *American Literature*, 31 (Jan. 1960), 446–455.

Graham, John. "Ernest Hemingway: The Meaning of Style." *Modern Fiction Studies*, 6 (Winter 1960), 298–313.

Hemingway, Ernest. *The Old Man and the Sea.* New York: Scribner's, 1952.

Young, Philip. *Ernest Hemingway.* New York: Rinehart, 1952.

————. *Ernest Hemingway*, Univ. of Minnesota Pamphlets on American Writers, No. 1. Minneapolis: Univ. of Minnesota Press, 1959.

9

Business and Social Letters

Writing letters is a necessary part of business and social life. Whether requesting an application form for college, seeking an adjustment on an improperly functioning product, thanking a friend for a gift, or expressing appreciation after a visit, the careful letter writer observes certain conventional standards. Further, the careful letter writer recognizes that his letter is a reflection of himself, and he tries to make it an individual communication. The thoughtful, well-written letter whose message is clear suggests a thoughtful and knowledgeable writer. The hasty, poorly written letter suggests a hasty, ill-informed writer. The form and content of the letter determines the recipient's impression of the writer and, hence, the effectiveness of the letter.

The first part of this chapter deals with business letters—their form (format, mechanics, and parts) and their content, particularly the letter of inquiry or request, the order letter, the adjustment letter, and the letter of application.

The second part of the section deals with social letters—their form and content, particularly the friendly letter, the thank-you letter, the bread-and-butter letter, and the letter of condolence.

BUSINESS LETTERS

Format and Mechanics

There are standard procedures concerning paper, typewriting, appearance, layout forms, and keeping a carbon copy of each letter. Failure to follow these standards shows very poor taste, reflects the ignorance of the writer, and invites an unfavorable response. In correspondence in the business world, there is no place for unusual or "cute" stylistic practices.

PAPER

Use unruled, good quality white paper, 8½-by-11 inches. Do not use notebook paper.

HANDWRITING OR TYPEWRITING

Business letters should be typewritten because typewriting is neater and easier to read. If a letter is handwritten, only black, blue, or blue-black ink should be used.

APPEARANCE

The general appearance of a letter is very important. A letter that is neat and pleasing to the eye invites reading and consideration much more readily than does one that is unbalanced or has noticeable erasures. The letter should be like a picture, framed on the page with margins in proportion to the length of the letter. Allow at least a 1½-inch margin at the top and bottom, and a 1-inch margin on the sides. Short letters should have wide margins and be appropriately centered on the page. As a general rule, single space within the parts of the letter; double space between the parts of the letter and between paragraphs. It is always a wise investment to spend an extra ten minutes to retype a letter if there is even the slightest doubt about its making a favorable impression on the reader. (See the letter on page 221 for proper spacing.)

LAYOUT FORMS

Although there are several standardized layout forms for business letters, two seem to be preferred by most firms: the block (see pages 221 and 230) and the modified block (see pages 226 and 228). In the block form the inside address, salutation, and paragraphs are flush, or even, with the left margin; the heading, complimentary close, and signature are to the right half of the page. The modified block differs in only one respect: each paragraph is indented.

CARBON COPY

Begin now to develop the wise habit of keeping a carbon copy of every business letter you send. The carbon copy records the address of the person written and the reason for the letter. Since more than one letter frequently is required in settling a matter, a carbon copy becomes a necessity for maintaining continuity in the correspondence.

Parts of a Business Letter

The parts of a business letter follow a standard sequence and arrangement. The six regular parts in the letter include: heading, inside address, salutation, body, complimentary close, and signature (these are illustrated in the letter on page 221). In addition, there may be several special parts in the business letter. The two parts on the envelope are the outside address and the return address (these are illustrated on page 224).

REGULAR PARTS OF THE LETTER

1. *Heading.* Located in the upper right-hand corner, the heading includes your complete mailing address and the date, in that order, as shown below. The longest line in the heading is flush, or even, with the right margin. As elsewhere in standard writing, abbreviations should generally be avoided.

704 South Pecan Circle   P.O. Box 408
Hanover, Pennsylvania 17331   Simmons College
April 9, 1971   Jasper, New York 11528
     1 January 1972

Many firms use stationery that has been especially printed for them with their name and address at the top of the page. Some firms have other information added to this *letterhead,* such as the names of officers, a telephone number, or a slogan. The letterhead on stationery is always put there by a printer. Thus, the writer of a business letter, whether a student or an employee, never makes his own letterhead by typing, writing, or drawing one in.

If letterhead stationery is used, only the date needs to be added. Generally, center the date directly under the letterhead or place it even with the right-hand margin. (See the letter on page 226.)

2. *Inside Address.* The inside address is placed even with the left margin and at least two spaces below the heading. It contains the full name of the person or firm being written to and the complete mailing address, as in the following illustration.

Mr. Fred A. Willis, President
Kipling Corporation
P.O. Box 127
Beverly Hills, California 90210

Preface a person's name with a title of respect, such as Miss, Mr., or Mrs. When addressing an official of a firm, follow his name with his title or position. Write a firm's name in exactly the same form that the firm itself uses. Although it may be difficult to find out the name of the person to whom a letter should be addressed, it is always better to address a letter to a specific person than to a title, office, or firm. In giving the street address, be sure to include the word *Street*, *Avenue*, *Circle*, etc. Remember, no abbreviations.

3. *Salutation.* The salutation, or greeting, is two spaces below the inside address and is even with the left margin. It is always followed by a colon. "Dear Sir:" and "Dear Mr. _____:" are the most often used salutations. When addressing a firm or a group of men, use "Gentlemen:"; use "Ladies:" for a group or firm of women. Use "Dear Miss _____:" for an unmarried woman, and "Dear Mrs. _____:" for a married woman. (Other feminine forms such as "Dear Madam:" and the plural "Madams:" or "Mesdames:" are seldom used in business letters.)

4. *Body.* The body, or the message, of the letter begins two spaces below the salutation. Like any other composition, it is structured in paragraphs. Generally, single space within paragraphs and double space between paragraphs. The paragraphs may or may not be indented, depending on the layout form used.

The wording of a business letter should be as natural and normal as possible. Avoid trying to sound impressive, for such an effort usually results in a stilted, awkward letter.

5. *Complimentary Close.* The complimentary close, or closing, is two spaces below the body and is slightly left of the center of the page. It is a conventional expression, indicating the formal close of the letter. Of the numerous possible expressions, "Yours truly," is always acceptable; less formal are "Yours very truly," "Very truly yours," "Sincerely," "Sincerely yours," and "Cordially." Capitalize only the first word, and always follow the complimentary close with a comma.

6. *Signature.* Every letter should have a legible, handwritten signature in ink. Four to six spaces below this is the typewritten signature. If the entire letter is handwritten, of course there is only one signature (see the letter on page 228).

A woman may include (Miss) or (Mrs.) in parentheses to the left of the typewritten signature (see the letter on page 228). In a business letter, a married woman uses her own first name, not her husband's first name. Thus, the wife of Jacob C. Andrews signs her name as Thelma S. Andrews. In addition, she may type her married name in parenthesis (Mrs. Jacob C. Andrews) below her own name.

The name of a firm as well as the name of the individual writing the letter may appear as the signature (see the letter on page 226). Responsibility for the letter's content rests with the name which appears first.

Following the typewritten signature there may be an identifying title indicating the position of the person signing the letter, such as President, Assistant to the Manager, or Director of Housing.

Special Parts of the Letter

In addition to the six regular parts of the business letter, sometimes special, or optional, parts are also necessary. The main ones, in the order in which they would appear in the letter, are the following.

1. *Attention Line.* When a letter is addressed to a company or organization rather than to an individual, an attention line may be given to help in mail delivery. An attention line is never used when the inside address contains a person's name. Typical attention lines are Sales Division, Personnel Manager, or Order Department; the attention line may also be an individual's name. The attention line contains the word *Attention* (capitalized and sometimes abbreviated) followed by a colon and name of the office, department, or individual. Examples:

> Attention: Personnel Manager
> Attn: Mr. Robbin Carmichael

The attention line appears both on the envelope and in the letter. On the envelope, it is generally two spaces below and an inch to the left of the address; frequently it is underlined. In the letter the

Regular Parts of the Business Letter and Their Spacing

At least 1½-inch margin at top

HEADING | Longest line determines left margin of heading

Route 3, Box 75
Elmhurst, Illinois 60126
July 25, 1971

Double space or more, depending on length of letter

INSIDE ADDRESS

Mr. Ronald M. Benrey
Fiction Editor, Experience
355 Lexington Avenue
New Sound, New York 10117

Same as address on envelope

Double space

SALUTATION Dear Mr. Benrey: Followed by colon

Double space

At least 1-inch margin on each side

BODY

In a creative writing course I am taking at Midwestern College, Elmhurst, Illinois, I have written several short stories that my instructor feels are worthy of publication. One of the stories won the first place fiction award in the recent Midwestern Literary Festival.

Double space

May I send you these short stories for your consideration for possible publication in Experience? I understand that you are quite interested in young writers.

Double space

COMPLIMENTARY CLOSE | Followed by comma; first word capitalized

Yours truly,

Closing and signature slightly left of center

4 to 6 spaces for handwritten signature

SIGNATURE

George Sankerton

At least 1½-inch margin at bottom

attention line is even with the left margin and is usually two spaces below the inside address. (See letters on pages 226 and 230.) Since a letter addressed to an individual is usually more effective than one addressed simply to a company, the attention line should be used sparingly.

2. *Subject or Reference Line.*   The subject, or reference, line saves time and space. It consists of the word *Subject* or *Re* (a Latin word meaning "concerning") followed by a colon and a word or phrase of specific information, such as a policy number, account number or model number. Examples:

> Subject: Policy No. 10473A
> Re: Latham Stereo Tape Deck Model 926

The position of the subject line is not standardized. It may appear to the right of the inside address or salutation; it may be centered on the page several spaces below the inside address; it may be even with the left margin and several spaces below the inside address; or it may be several spaces below the salutation.

3. *Identification Line.*   When the person whose signature appears on the letter is not the person who typed the letter, there is an identification line. It is made up of two sets of initials separated by a colon: the initials of the sender (usually capitalized) followed by the initials of the typist (usually lower case). Example:

> RJP:jh   or   rjp:jh

The identification line is two spaces below the signature and is even with the left margin of the letter. (See letter on page 226.)

4. *Enclosure.*   When an item (pamphlet, report, checks, etc.) is enclosed with the letter, usually an enclosure line is typed two spaces below the identification line and even with the left margin. If there is no identification line, the enclosure line is two spaces below the signature and even with the left margin. The enclosure line may be written in various ways and may give varying amounts of information. Examples:

> Enclosure
> Enclosures: Inventory of Supplies, Furniture and Equipment

> Monthly report of absenteeism, sick leave, and
> vacation leave

Encl. (2)
(See letters on pages 226 and 228.)

5. *Carbon Copy.* When a carbon copy of the letter is sent to another person, the letters *cc* (usually lower case) followed by a colon
and his name are typed one space below the identification line and
even with the left margin of the letter. If there is no identification
line, the carbon copy notation is two spaces below the signature and
even with the left margin. Example:

cc: Mr. Jay Longman

6. *Personal Line.* The word *Personal* or *Confidential* (capitalized
and usually underlined) indicates that only the addressee is to read
the letter; obviously, this line should appear on the envelope. It
usually appears to the left of the last line of the outside address. The
personal line may be included in the letter itself, two spaces above
the inside address and even with the left margin.

Parts on the Envelope

REGULAR PARTS ON THE ENVELOPE

The two regular parts on the envelope, the outside address and
the return address, are explained below and illustrated on page 224.

1. *Outside Address.* Except for possible double spacing, the outside address on the envelope is identical with the inside address. If
the outside address is more than three lines, single space; otherwise
double space for ease in reading. For obvious reasons, the address
should be accurate and complete.

2. *Return Address.* Located in the upper left-hand corner of the
envelope, not on the back on the flap, the return address includes
your name (without "Mr.") plus your address as it appears in the
heading.

SPECIAL PARTS ON THE ENVELOPE

In addition to the two regular parts on the envelope, sometimes
a special part is needed. The main ones are the attention line and
the personal line.

Regular Parts of the Envelope and Their Spacing

RETURN ADDRESS	George Sankerton Route 3, Box 75 Elmhurst, Illinois 60126	*Except for name and date same as heading in letter*
	Begin outside address slightly below and left of center	
OUTSIDE ADDRESS	*Same as inside address in letter*	Mr. Ronald M. Benrey Fiction Editor, <u>Experience</u> 355 Lexington Avenue New Sound, New York 10117

1. *Attention Line.* An attention line may be used when a letter is addressed to a company rather than to an individual. The wording of the attention line on the envelope is the same as that of the attention line in the letter. On the envelope, the attention line is generally two spaces below and about an inch to the left of the outside address; frequently it is underlined.

2. *Personal Line.* The word *Personal* or *Confidential* (capitalized and usually underlined) indicates that only the addressee is to read the letter. The personal line usually appears to the left of the last line of the outside address.

CONTENT OF BUSINESS LETTERS

The basic principles of composition apply to business letters as they do to any other form of writing. You should have clearly in mind the purpose of the letter and its intended reader, and you should carefully organize the sentences and paragraphs so that they say what you want them to say.

The business letter, however, differs from the other forms of composition discussed in this handbook in one major, overriding respect; in the business letter there is one intended reader who is named and to whom the communication is specifically addressed.

This makes the business letter more personal. Courtesy becomes important, and the "you" of the letter is stressed. This "you" attitude is achieved by emphasizing qualities of the addressee and by minimizing references to "I," "me," "my," "we," and "us."

Letters concerned with inquiry, order, adjustment, and job application are discussed on the following pages.

Letter of Inquiry or Request

A letter to the college registrar asking for entrance information, a letter to a firm asking for a copy of its catalog, a letter to a manufacturing plant requesting information on a particular product—each is a letter of inquiry, or request. (See the letter on page 221.) Such a letter is simple to write if these directions are followed:

> State clearly and specifically what is wanted.
> Give the reason for the inquiry.
> Include an expression of appreciation for the addressee's consideration of the inquiry.

The Order Letter

The order letter, as the term implies, is a written communication to a seller from a buyer who wishes to make a purchase. (See the letter on page 226.) For the transaction to be satisfactory, the terms of the sale must be absolutely clear to both. Since in the order letter it is the writer (purchaser) who is requesting that certain merchandise be delivered to him, it is his responsibility to state clearly, completely, and accurately exactly what he wants, how he will pay for it, and how he wants it delivered.

The letter must be as specific as possible in its description of the merchandise being ordered. This specific description should include the exact name of the item, the quantity wanted, and other identifying information, such as model number, catalog number, size, color, weight, and finish.

Whether the order letter involves only a few dollars or many thousands, the money is important. The price of the merchandise and the method of payment (check, money order, credit card, C.O.D., or charge to account if credit is established) should be clearly stated.

Include shipping instructions with the order. Indicate by what means (parcel post, truck freight, railway freight, Railway Express, or air express) the merchandise is to be delivered. If the date of shipment is important, say so.

Order Letter in Modified Block Form on Letterhead Stationery

JOHNSON YARD SERVICE

Telephone 743-842-7166   P.O. Box 431
Browning, Texas 77020

June 1, 1971

Arlington Manufacturing Company, Inc.
1149 Seventh Avenue
Deevers, Ohio 44109

Attention: Parts Replacement Department

Gentlemen:

Please mail me a 19-inch flat cutting blade
for a series "W" lawn mower. Enclosed is a check
for $3.25 for the part.

I am greatly in need of the blade and would
appreciate your sending it by first class mail.
Please bill me for any additional postage above
the postpaid cost of the blade.

Yours truly,
JOHNSON YARD SERVICE

Thomas C. Johnson

Thomas C. Johnson

TCJ:mj
Enclosure: Check for $3.25

The Adjustment Letter

The letter seeking adjustment is in some ways the most difficult to write. Frequently, the writer is angry or annoyed or extremely dissatisfied and his first impulse is to express his feelings in a harsh, angry, sarcastic letter. But the purpose of the adjustment letter is to bring about positive action that satisfies the complaint. A rude letter that antagonizes the reader seldom results in such positive action. Thus, above all in writing an adjustment letter, be calm, courteous, and businesslike. Assume that the reader is fair and reasonable. Include only factual information, not opinions; and keep the focus on the real issue, not on personalities.

Generally, the adjustment letter includes these three points: (1) identification of the transaction, (2) statement of the problem, and (3) desired action.

The adjustment letter on page 228 illustrates a common complaint: a recently purchased appliance is not operating properly.

The Letter of Application

The most important letter a person ever writes may well be a letter of application for a job. Since there are usually several applicants for a position, the letter might be the decisive factor, particularly in whether or not an interview is granted. And the letter of application is successful if it results in an interview.

ORGANIZATION

The letter of application has three sections: purpose of the letter, background information, and request for an interview. The background information may be included entirely within the letter itself or it may be given on a separate page, referred to as "Data Sheet," "Personal Information," or some similar title. Regardless of how the background information is presented, however, the purpose of the letter is stated in the first paragraph, and an interview is requested in the closing paragraph.

Purpose of the Letter. In the first paragraph state that the letter is an application for a job (it is usually better to apply for a specific position than for an "opening"). Tell how you found out about the job, and explain your reason for wanting it.

Background Information. This section of one or more paragraphs includes personal data, education, experience, and references,

Adjustment Letter Handwritten in Modified Block Form

7820 Cohn Street
New Orleans
Lousiana 70118
January 4, 1972

Helen Gallagher - Foster House
6523 North Galena Road
Peoria, Illinois 61601

Ladies :

As the enclosed papers will show, I recently ordered from you an electric refrigerator defroster, Item No. 6392, costing $3.99. A few days ago when I used the defroster for the first time, it worked perfectly for the first five minutes or so; then it unexplainably stopped giving off heat. Your catalog states that every item is guaranteed 100 percent or the purchaser's money is refunded. Therefore, I am returning the defective defroster to you with the request that it be replaced. I much prefer to have a refrigerator defroster - that works - than to have the $3.99.

It is always a pleasure to look through your catalogs, and for a number of years I have enjoyed various products from you. I trust that you will make the necessary adjustments concerning the electric refrigerator defroster.

Sincerely yours,

(Miss) Suzanne Yates

Enclosures

with emphasis on the qualities that would be most useful in fulfilling the job being sought. Personal data include such items as age, height, weight, condition of health, physical disabilities, marital status and dependents, and military status. Include in the letter *only* those items that apply to the job.

Educational background includes information about both the high school and the college attended: name and location, date of graduation, areas of emphasis or of particular interest, awards or special recognition, and important extracurricular activities. In the letter, concentrate on the courses, activities, and other learning experiences that would contribute to doing the prospective job well.

Work experience is a list of all previous jobs, beginning with the most recent or present one. For each job, give the date of employment, the specific work, the name and address of the firm, and the full name of the supervisor. Stress the work experiences that are relevant to the job being applied for.

The final part of the background information is the listing of three to five references, persons who can vouch for your character and ability. These should include at least a person who has known you for a long time, a former employer, and a teacher. Give the full name of each individual and his complete business address, and indicate in what capacity he knows you. Ask permission before using a person's name as a reference; in asking such permission, it is wise to state the job being applied for. If especially eager to get a particular job, it might be helpful to ask each of these persons to write a letter of recommendation to reach the prospective employer shortly after the application does.

Request for an Interview.   Any firm interested in employing an applicant will want to interview him. In the closing paragraph of the letter of application, therefore, request an interview at the prospective employer's convenience. However, should there be restrictions on your time, such as classes or work, say so. If distance makes an interview impractical (for instance, living in Virginia and applying for a summer job in Yellowstone National Park), suggest some alternative, such as an interview with a local representative. As a final word, be sure to include in this closing paragraph how and when you may be reached.

The following is an example of a letter of application.

Letter of Application in Block Form

516 North Madison Street
Jackson, Mississippi 39207
March 3, 1972

Ratliff Construction Company
Union
Tennessee   38014

Attention: Director of Personnel

Dear Sir:

Through Tom Spengler, who worked with your company last summer and plans to again this summer,
I have learned that you are hiring a number of
additional college students for summer work.
I would like to apply for a job as a general construction worker.

I am 19 years old, 5 feet 10 inches tall, and
weigh 175 pounds. I am in excellent health and
am able to do strenuous physical work. In high
school I lettered in football two years. Presently, I am a freshman at Hinds Junior College,
majoring in architecture. On Saturdays and during
the summer for the past three years I have worked
in a neighborhood grocery store. Mr. Douglas
R. Grant, owner of Grant's Grocery, 903 North
Madison Street, Jackson, Mississippi 39207, told
me he would be happy to write a letter of recommendation for me. If you wish further references,
please contact Mr. Charles A. Wadman, Instructor
of Drafting and Design Technology, Hinds Junior
College, Raymond, Mississippi 39154, or a neighbor, Mr. J. R. Russum, 4432 Timmes Avenue, Jackson, Mississippi 39213.

Your company, I understand, specializes in the
construction of apartment buildings. Since apartment design has been particularly appealing to me
in college this year, I am very interested in
working for your company. May I come to Union
for an interview? Our spring holidays are only a
few weeks away, April 7-17, and I could very con-
veniently come any day during that period. Or
if I knew at least two weeks ahead of time so that
I could make arrangements about my work at the
grocery, I could drive up any Saturday. I can
usually be reached at my home address before
7:30 A.M. and after 4:00 P.M., and my telephone
number is 601-254-7613. I will be looking forward
to hearing from you.

                    Sincerely yours,

                    Albert L. Livingston

Letter Accepting or Declining a Job Offer

Closely related to the letter of application is the letter accepting
or declining a job offer. When the letter of application and the interview are successful and a job is offered, the letter of response is
very important. If accepting the job, you want to continue the good
impression already made on the new employer. And if declining a
job, it is simply good business to do so tactfully and courteously.

The acceptance letter is primarily a matter of form. Name the
specific position, state that you accept the job and when you will
begin work, and offer appreciation for the favorable consideration
of the application.

The following is the body of a letter accepting the job applied
for in the above letter.

Thank you for your letter of April 23 offering me a summer job as a general construction worker with your company. I accept this job and will report to your office for crew assignment at 8:00 A.M. on June 1.

This summer promises to be particularly valuable for me. By working for one of the most reputable construction companies in this area, I will have opportunity to see the practical application of many of the things I have been studying in my courses as an architecture major.

I am looking forward to starting to work on June 1.

The letter declining a job offer requires tact and courtesy. Cultivate goodwill and keep open the lines of communication that have been established. Although you are declining a job today, you may well be seeking permanent employment with the same company at some later date.

In the letter declining a job offer, mention the job, state that the job is declined, give a valid reason, and show appreciation for the favorable consideration of the application. Write the letter promptly, and, as in all business letters, maintain a "business" tone.

Below is the body of a letter declining the job applied for in the letter on pages 230–231.

Thank you for your letter of April 23 offering me a summer job as a general construction worker with your company. I regret that I am unable to accept the job. Since the interview with you on April 13, a football knee injury has been reactivated, and I am scheduled to have surgery just as soon as I finish my final exams. My doctor instructs me that I am to do no strenuous physical work during the summer if he is to guarantee me that my knee will be as good as new.

Not being able to accept this job is a real disappointment to me. I had looked forward to working for one of the most reputable construction companies in this area and to seeing the practical application of many of the things I have been studying in my courses as an architecture major.

SOCIAL LETTERS

The social letter is the form of composition that probably most people (students and nonstudents, men and women alike) use more often than any other. From the standpoint of sheer practicality, then, a study of social letter-writing—however brief—is time well spent. Because social letters represent you to your friends and affect their estimate of you, such letters deserve your thoughtful attention. Social letters follow sound writing principles. A well-written social letter is no more a collection of disjointed statements than is a well-written theme. For all of these reasons, you should know the conventional practices for writing social letters.

The general discussion that follows deals with the form and content of the types of social letters written most often: the friendly letter, the thank-you letter, the bread-and-butter letter, and the letter of condolence. For a detailed discussion of acceptable practices in social correspondence, consult the standard books of etiquette (such as those by Emily Post or by Amy Vanderbilt) available in any library.

Stationery

For social letters use unruled, good quality stationery in a neutral shade (such as white, gray, tan, or blue).

Handwriting or Typewriting

Typewriting is permissible, even encouraged if your handwriting is poor, for almost all social letters. A condolence letter, however, should always be handwritten. For all social letters a conservative color of ink (blue, blue-black, or black) is always appropriate. Whether the letter is typewritten or handwritten, the signature should be handwritten.

Parts of the Social Letter

The five parts of a social letter (except the heading) follow a standard sequence and arrangement. Generally, single space within each part and double space between the parts and between paragraphs.

1. *Heading.* The heading is the least standardized part in the social letter. As in the business letter, it may be located in the upper right-hand corner and may include the sender's complete mailing address and the date. (See the letter on page 236.) The sender's address, however, is often omitted if it is well known to the addressee. (See the letter on page 237.) The date line too is flexible: the year

may be omitted and the date may appear below and to the left of the signature. (See the letter on page 238.)

2. *Salutation.* The salutation, or greeting, is even with the left margin. It is always followed by a comma. The salutation is usually the word "Dear" (capitalized) plus the addressee's name: "Dear Bob," or "Dear Sarah Ann."

3. *Body.* The body, or the message, of the letter begins two spaces below the salutation. Indent each paragraph, single space within the paragraph, and double space between paragraphs.

4. *Complimentary Close.* The complimentary close, or closing, is centered two spaces below the body. A conventional expression, it is always capitalized (only the first word) and followed by a comma. Typical closings are "Sincerely," "Love," "Cordially," and "Affectionately."

5. *Signature.* The signature is indented below the complimentary close. Usually the first name is sufficient; however, if the first name alone would confuse the addressee, the last name should be added for clarity.

Parts of the Envelope

As in the business letter, the envelope of the social letter has two parts: the outside address and the return address.

1. *Outside Address.* The outside address is composed of the addressee's name and complete mailing address. Obviously, it should be written clearly and accurately. In addressing adults, the name should be preceded by an appropriate title (Mrs., Mr., Miss, Dr., etc.). In addressing a boy up to age twelve, use the title "Master"; for a teenage boy use no title; for a male eighteen years and above, use "Mr." For a girl, from birth to marriage, "Miss" is the proper title.

2. *Return Address.* The return address is composed of your name and complete mailing address. Although the post office department prefers that the return address be in the upper left-hand corner on the face of the envelope, personalized stationery usually has the return address on the flap. A man does not precede his name with "Mr."; a married woman uses her husband's name (Mrs. John Smith,

rather than Mrs. Rebecca Smith); and an unmarried woman uses "Miss" before her name.

CONTENT OF SOCIAL LETTERS

As in other forms of writing, you should keep in mind the intended reader and the purpose for writing. Each social letter is written to a specific person for a specific reason. For example, a thank-you letter to an employer for a wedding gift would differ in tone and emphasis from a friendly letter written to a college roommate during summer vacation.

The Friendly Letter

Everyone enjoys receiving letters from friends, particularly letters that include interesting and newsy details. Such letters are not difficult to write, although at the same time they should not be dashed off in a few hurried seconds.

The friendly letter is a one-way conversation on paper. Naturally its content, varying in length from a few lines to several pages, primarily reflects the thoughts and actions of the writer. If there is difficulty in knowing how to begin or what to say, imagine the presence of the friend. Tell him in the letter what you would say to him in a conversation.

Make the letter colorful and delightful to read by including specific details. Consider, for instance, the two following paragraphs.

> We had a great time on our vacation in New Orleans. We saw all the sights and ate at several famous restaurants. We were busy doing something every minute of the two weeks we were there.

> We had a great time on our vacation in New Orleans. One of our excursions was a boat trip on the *Voyageur* into Cajun country. We passed the alleged hiding place of the pirate Jean Laffite's loot, and on many of the bayous we saw Cajuns of all ages fishing. One little fellow who couldn't have been more than ten had a string of catfish that would feed our family for a month. After seeing the skin of a fourteen-foot alligator at the trading post, I really watched my step!

The first paragraph is made up entirely of generalities, and thus is rather dull reading. The second paragraph, on the other hand, gives specific details that permit the reader to share in the writer's experience.

The Thank-you Letter

The thank-you letter, as the term implies, is an expression of appreciation, usually for a gift. Such a letter is obligatory if a gift were mailed or were in honor of an occasion such as graduation or marriage.

Write the thank-you letter promptly. Mention the gift by name and make the thank you sincere. The letter need not be long, but its recipient should feel that his effort and expense in selecting the gift are appreciated.

Avoid sending as a thank-you letter a commercial card that already has the message printed inside. Such cards lack the personal touch essential to a sincere thank you.

The following is an example of a thank-you letter.

347 Oriole Road
Otto, Michigan 49012
June 15, 1971

Dear Aunt Sue and Uncle Hank,

The rod and reel you gave me for graduation from junior college is more fun than anything I've ever owned. A couple of the fellows here on the farm where I'm working are real fishing pros, and we three have been trying out the nearby streams. I wish you could have seen that speckled trout I reeled in yesterday afternoon.

Your nephew,

Billy

The Bread-and-Butter Letter

The bread-and-butter letter, a type of thank-you letter, is written to the hostess after an overnight stay as a guest. The well-written bread-and-butter letter is prompt, friendly, sincere, and graceful, as illustrated below.

March 13

Dear Dianne,

The visit in your home, as always, was both relaxing and stimulating. Attending painting class with you and dabbling for the first time in oils has opened a new world to me. In fact, on the way home yesterday, I stopped at the hobby shop that you recommended and bought a beginner's oil painting kit.

Affectionately,

The Letter of Condolence

The letter of condolence, handwritten on plain white stationery, is an expression of sympathy when a person has died. A short, simple note addressed to the nearest relative of the deceased is often of comfort to the bereaved family. In writing the condolence letter, be sincere and natural, avoiding a morbid tone.

Here is an example of a letter of condolence.

Dear Sally—
I was indeed saddened to learn
of your brother's tragic automobile
accident. Although I did not know

him, I felt his vivacious influence every time you recounted with such enthusiasm experiences of your childhood and of your high school years together.

Please know, Sally, that my heart and my thoughts are with you and with your family.

Very sincerely,
Jean Meyers

September 15

Glossary

active voice: The verb form that indicates the subject is acting and that is always followed by a direct object.

adjective: A word used to describe, limit, or qualify a noun or pronoun.

adjective clause: A dependent word group containing a subject-verb relationship and used to modify a noun or pronoun.

adverb: A word used to modify a verb, an adjective, or another adverb.

adverb clause: A dependent word group containing a subject-verb relationship and used to modify a verb, an adjective, or another adverb.

adverbial noun: A noun used to tell "where?" "when?" and "how much?" *Example:* I walked *home* from work. (Tells where)

antecedent: "That which goes before." It is a term identifying the word or words to which a pronoun refers. *Example:* After finishing *their* classwork, the *students* began work on *their* lab assignments. (The antecedent of pronoun "their" is "students.")

appositive: A word added to a noun or pronoun to explain it; it gives another name for the noun or pronoun. *Example:* The vernier caliper, a precision *instrument*, is used by the machinist.

auxiliary verb: A word that helps a verb to make a statement, ask a question, or give a command. Common auxiliaries are forms of "do," "have" and "be," "shall," "will."

case: A term used in reference to pronouns and sometimes to nouns. The three cases are nominative, possessive, and objective. Each case identifies a group of forms that have defined uses within the sentence.

clause: A group of words, including at least a subject-verb relationship, that may be a complete sentence or only part of a sentence. If a complete sentence, the group of words is identified as an independent or principal clause. If only a part of a sentence, the group is a dependent or subordinate clause (either noun, adjective, or adverb, depending on use in the sentence). *Examples:* In technical drawing, accuracy, speed, and neatness are essential. (*Independent clause*). *When you say you weigh 160 pounds*, you are saying the earth and you attract each other mutually with a force of 160 pounds. (*Dependent clause*)

comparison: A term used to indicate degrees of adjective and adverb forms. The three degrees of comparison are positive, comparative, and superlative.

complex sentence: A sentence containing one independent clause and one or more dependent clauses. *Example:* A body possessing kinetic energy does work (*independent clause*) when it is stopped or slowed down (*dependent clause*).

compound sentence: A sentence containing two or more independent clauses usually joined by a stated coordinate conjunction or a semicolon. *Example:* Decisions on granting credit are made by the treasurer (*independent clause*), *and* accounting procedures are established by the controller (*independent clause*).

conjunction: A part of speech used to connect or join words, phrases, and clauses. Simple coordinate conjunctions are used to connect words, phrases, and clauses of equal rank ("and," "but," "or," "nor," "for," "yet," "so"). Correlative conjunctions are used to connect words, phrases, and clauses of equal rank ("not only . . . but also," "both . . . and," "either . . . or," "neither . . . nor"). Conjunctive adverbs link independent clauses ("however," "moreover," "thus"). Subordinate conjunctions are used to introduce dependent clauses that are subordinate to the rest of the sentence ("as," "since," "because," "when," "after").

conjunctive adverb: An adverb used as a connective to link two independent clauses. Common ones are "however," "also," "therefore," "nevertheless," "consequently."

declarative sentence: A sentence that makes a statement. (See "independent clause" and "simple sentence.") *Example:* I am majoring in design.

demonstrative adjective: "This," "that," "these," "those" when used to modify substantives. *Example: These* machines will soon have to be replaced.

demonstrative pronoun: A pronoun that indicates or points out ("this," "that," "these," "those"). *Example: This* is my classroom.

dependent clause: A group of words containing at least a subject-verb relationship but unable to stand alone. The dependent clause is subordinate to the main clause; actually it "depends" on the main clause to complete its meaning. The dependent clause may be adjective, adverb, or noun, depending on its use in the sentence.

direct address: A term describing a construction in which a person or persons is called by name. *Examples: Mr. Lewis,* may I answer the question? *Class,* open your books to Chapter 1.

direct object: The word or phrase following the verb and receiving the action identified by the verb. *Example:* When using a hammer, always grasp the *handle* at the extreme end.

gerund: A verbal form always ending in "-ing" and used as a noun.

helper verb: See "auxiliary verb."

imperative sentence: A sentence that issues a command or order. The subject of the sentence ("you" is understood) is in the second person. *Example:* Close that door.

indefinite pronoun: A pronoun indicating any one or more of a class of things, rather than one particular thing: "everyone," "any," "some."

independent clause: A group of words containing at least a subject-verb relationship and capable of standing alone. It makes an independent assertion. *Example:* One form of decentralization is profit decentralization.

indirect object: A noun or pronoun following the verb to answer to whom or for whom the action of the verb is done. *Example:* Give *him* his assignment.

infinitive: A verb form made up of the first principal part of the verb plus "to," either expressed or understood. *Examples:* Let me *show* you the fastest method ("to" understood). We were asked *to construct* a building of aluminum.

interjection: A part of speech indicating sudden or strong feeling. It has no grammatical relationship to the sentence following, if there is one. *Examples:* Help! Ouch! Oh, dear, the door is stuck.

interrogative pronoun: A pronoun used in asking a question: "who," "what," "whose," "which." *Example: Who* is your instructor?

interrogative sentence: A sentence that asks a question. *Example:* Where is the tape?

intransitive verb: A verb form whose subject neither acts nor receives action. *Example:* The unit *runs* continuously.

linking verb: A term identifying such verbs as "be," "appear," "seem," "become," "taste," "feel," etc., that join or link subject and subjective complement. *Examples:* John *is* ill. Sometimes workers *become* careless.

mood: Identifies three verb forms: the indicative, the subjunctive, and the imperative. These forms identify specific ways verb forms are used in making statements and asking questions, expressing a wish or uncertainty, or giving commands.

noun: Traditionally, a part of speech naming a person, place, thing, quality, collection, or action. Also a word adding an affix to show number (affixes "s" or "es" to form plural) and possession (affixes " 's" " ' ").

object: See "direct object," and "indirect object."

objective complement: A word following the direct object to tell something about it: usually describes or renames the direct object. *Examples:* We elected him *chairman.* (Renames) The committee judged his entry *superior.* (Describes)

participle: A verb form ending in "-ing," "-ed," "-en," and sometimes indicated by a change in form as in "sung," used as an adjective. *Example:* The offset screwdriver has two blades *positioned* at right angles to each other.

passive voice: The verb form that indicates the subject is acted upon. The passive-voice verb includes a form of the verb "be" plus the third principal part of a main verb. *Example:* Screwdrivers *are made* with blades of various widths.

person: A term identifying whether person referred to speaks, is spoken to, or is spoken of. *Examples: I* performed the experiment. (*First person—speaks*). Did *you* perform the experiment? (*Second person— spoken to*). He performed the experiment (*Third person—spoken of*)

phrase: A group of words containing *no* subject-verb relationship; the group of words acts as a grammatical unit. *Examples:* Administrative authority consists *of certain permissions or rights.* (*Prepositional phrase*). *To convert from one given dimensional unit to another,* use the conversion factor method. (*Infinitive phrase*). *Assigning authority* is not simple. (*Gerund phrase*). The theory *had been satisfactorily proved.* (*Verb phrase*)

predicate: See "verb."

predicate adjective: An adjective following the verb and describing the subject. See "subjective complement" and "linking verb." *Examples:* For exterior walls of houses a pale gray color is *pleasant.* The experiment seemed *easy.*

predicate noun: A noun following the linking verb, completing its meaning. It renames the subject. See "subjective complement" and "linking verb." *Examples:* The manometer is a measuring *device.*

preposition: A word indicating the relationship between the noun that follows and some other word in the sentence. Common prepositions: "to," "in," "by," "for," "at," "near," "into," "through," "of," before," "after."

prepositional phrase: The preposition, its object, and any modifiers.

principal clause: See "independent clause."

principal parts: The basic forms of the verb used to form all other tenses. Basic forms include the present (first principal part), the past (second principal part), and the past participle (third principal part).

pronoun: A word used in the place of a noun.

relative pronoun: Relative pronouns ("who," "whom," "whose," "which," "that," "what") are used both to join dependent adjective clauses to the independent clause and to function within the adjective clause as subject, direct object, or object of preposition. (*Note:* "Who," "whom," "whose," and "that" refer to people; "which," "that," and "what" refer to animals and things.) *Example:* Gray, *which is produced by mixing black and white,* has no particular character of its own. ("Which" both introduces the adjective clause and serves as its subject.)

simple sentence: An independent clause that makes a single assertion. See "independent clause."

subject: A word or phrase that identifies what the sentence is about. *Examples:* A *bench vice* is commonly used to hold the workpiece. *Learning to convert Centrigrade to Fahrenheit* can be difficult.

subjective complement: A word or phrase following the verb that completes the meaning of the verb. The word either describes or renames the subject. See "predicate adjective" and "predicate noun."

subordinate clause: See "dependent clause."

subordinate conjunction: Words used to introduce dependent clauses and to connect the clause to the independent clause. Common subordinate conjunctions are "where," "when," "as," "since," "because," "unless," "after," "before," "although."

substantive: A term applied to a noun or any word or group of words equivalent to a noun.

tense: A term used to identify the time of action of the verb.

transitive verb: An action verb. The subject of the verb either acts or receives the action. *Examples:* He *drove* the car. (Subject acts). The car *was driven*. (Subject receives the action).

verb: Words that help make statements, ask questions, or give commands; words that change form to denote tense.

voice: Term used in reference to verbs: indicates whether the subject is acting (active voice) or being acted upon (passive voice). *Examples:* The student *repaired* the cooling unit. (*Active*) The cooling unit *was repaired* by the student. (*Passive*)

Index